DATE DUE

DEMCO, INC. 38-2931

Career Launcher

Internet

Career Launcher series

Career Launcher

Internet

Lisa McCoy

Ferguson Publishing
An imprint of Infobase Publishing

Career Launcher: Internet

Ferguson
An imprint of Infobase Publishing
132 West 31st Street
New York NY 10001

Library of Congress Cataloging-in-Publication Data

McCoy, Lisa.
    Internet / Lisa McCoy.
        p. cm. — (Career launcher series)
    Includes bibliographical references and index.
    ISBN-13: 978-0-8160-7951-3 (hardcover : alk. paper)
    ISBN-10: 0-8160-7951-X (hardcover : alk. paper)
1. Web sites—Design—Vocational guidance—Juvenile literature.
2. Electronic commerce—Vocational guidance—Juvenile literature. I. Title.
    TK5105.888.M37523 2009
    006.7023—dc22

                                                                    2010011887

Produced by Print Matters, Inc.
Text design by A Good Thing, Inc.
Cover design by Takeshi Takahashi
Cover printed by Yurchak Printing, Landisville, Penn.
Book printed and bound by Yurchak Printing, Landisville, Penn.
Date printed: April 2011

Printed in the United States of America

10 9 8 7 6 5 4 3 2 1

This book is printed on acid-free paper.

Contents

Foreword

Work is hard and navigating a career, even harder. (If it were easy it would not be called work!) But resources are available to help you. This book is one of them; and the fact that you are reading this speaks well of your motivation and desire to take control of your future, traits that will serve you well throughout your career.

At this point in your career you may not know what you want to do, how to begin, or where you will end up. That is very normal; do not fret. When I began my career on the Internet in 1994, the commercialized Web was just beginning to emerge. A company called Netscape had just released the first "popular" Web browser and, for all intents and purposes, the Web as we know it was born. Armed with a degree in U.S. history, the only thing I knew for sure about my career was that I would not pursue a career in U.S. history! Like many recent college grads, I had no idea what I wanted to do.

I moved to New York to be with my then-girlfriend (and now wife) and responded to a classified ad in the *New York Times* for "Mac People Needed." While I may not have known where my career would take me, I was immediately drawn to the notion of earning a paycheck for spending time on a computer—in any capacity. That job turned out to be converting mail-order print catalogs onto CD-ROM, and soon after, onto the Web. We were quite literally one of the first e-commerce companies, although there was no actual purchasing in the early days—just product browsing online. I could not have known then that those three words, *Mac People Needed*, would set me along the path I would follow ever since.

The lessons are clear: as you start out on your career, *follow your interests regardless of where they take you.* You will spend a good portion of your day working at your job; better to spend it on something you enjoy than something you hate. *Do not be afraid to experiment.* Did I know that my first job would be with one of the first e-commerce companies, or that it would lead to a lasting career on the Internet? Definitely not! But I was willing to experiment and it paid off. Similarly, *waiting for the perfect job is not necessarily the best approach*, as you may not know what perfect is until you are doing it. A "perfect" experience is one where you can learn and develop new skills in an environment that shares your values, respects your contributions, and compensates you fairly. If you can combine this with a great boss and/or mentor with room for advancement, you have found the perfect job, irrespective of the actual company. When you hit a ceiling, stop learning, the environment changes, or the compensation does not keep pace with your contributions, it is time to move on. It is through this boom-and-bust cycle that your career will emerge. Find jobs in fields you enjoy, learn, grow, and move on. That is how most careers are formed.

What makes the Internet unique as a career is that it offers something for everyone. Nearly every industry and every job function has an Internet counterpart: marketing, sales, product development, engineering, finance, human resources, business development, and so on. Each of these functions play a role in traditional industries, in Internet-related companies, and in traditional companies requiring Internet-related skills. A career on the Internet can take you just about anywhere, even more of a reason to choose jobs that interest you.

Another unique factor is that the Internet continues to emerge while leaving defined standards in its wake. The benefit to job seekers is that if you are looking to plug into an established job with defined roles, responsibilities, and performance metrics, you will find an Internet job right for you. Online marketers can develop skills in established areas like search engine marketing or search engine optimization, and track their performance against CPM, cost per click, user acquisition, and so on. Project managers can develop formal skills in various project management methodologies, such as Agile, Waterfall, Prince2, and so on.

On the other end of the spectrum, if you are looking for a job with less structure, less precedent, and room to pave new ground, there is no more expansive environment than the Internet. Online marketers can join emerging fields like social-network marketing or mobile marketing. Project managers can blaze new trails on next generation mobile e-commerce platforms, cloud computing resources, or the next worker-productivity tools. The opportunities are truly limitless.

Before I leave you to Lisa's book, which is an absolutely fantastic resource for tips, tools, and information that can help you land your ideal job, I have a few more words of advice that have served me well throughout my career and may be meaningful to you, regardless of job or industry.

First, work hard. Sounds obvious, but I mean it. Push yourself, push your limits. Be the first to the office and the last to leave. Work on weekends. Do whatever it takes to stand out. Develop a reputation as the hardest worker in your company. Even if it is an entry-level job full of administrative tasks—do them quickly, do them well, and volunteer for more. Let people know that they can count on you. You may not be the smartest person at your company or even the best at what you do—but there is always a place for people who work hard. And if you happen to be the smartest or best at what you do, combine that with a strong work ethic and you will surely go far.

Kill your coworkers with kindness. Do your job with a smile on your face. There will always be some reason to complain; an annoying coworker, a mean boss, questionable management decisions. Keep your head above the fray and stay away from the gossip. Again, strive to be the one that everyone can count on—even if you are the one with the bad boss. Even bad bosses need employees that they can count on, and that person will not be your boss forever, so try and suck it up until you are ready to move on.

Find a mentor. Ideally this will be your boss, but not necessarily. A good mentor is someone who has been there before and is willing to take the time to help you get through your difficult issues. They can help you navigate the politics of the workplace and, if you are lucky, can help you with your advancement through the organization.

Do not bottleneck or gate-keep critical information. If you are given responsibility for a system or process that other people in the business rely upon, share information with them. Make it easy for them to use the system, not more difficult because it makes you feel more important. Any time you can make it easier for coworkers to do their jobs they will respect you far more than if you make them feel beholden to you.

Read everything you can about your industry and your job function. Know as much as you can and continue to develop your skills. Read industry blogs, magazines, Web sites, subscribe to RSS feeds, follow industry leaders on Twitter, Google Buzz, and so on. And read books (like this one!).

Build your network, online and offline. Go to industry events. Have drinks with coworkers after work and on weekends. Make the effort to make friends with coworkers because they will become your best network as you each move on in your careers. And on that note, do not burn any bridges—even if things do not work out for you at a given job.

Own and cultivate your personal brand. Start a blog, Tweet, share yourself and your insights. Leave comments on other blogs.

The Internet gives you an unparalleled medium to establish and manage your reputation. Your online reputation can be far more valuable than your résumé.

Lastly, find your passion. If you do not know what it is yet, then take jobs that are interesting to you and keep searching until you find it. It may take years before you know what it is, and that is okay. Keep searching. Take jobs that are interesting to you, work hard, learn as much as you can and then use this book to help you move on to the next thing. You will eventually find it and when you do, you too will be able to look back upon your successful career on the Internet and share your experiences like I was able to do here. Happy reading and best of luck as you embark upon your career!

— Corey Podolsky
VICE PRESIDENT OF STRATEGIC PARTNERSHIPS
ENTOURAGE SYSTEMS, INC.

Acknowledgments

The author would like to gratefully acknowledge the following people for their repeated willingness to share their experience and insights—their help was truly invaluable: Renee Barnaby, Michael Jensen, Ed McKillop, Chris Palma, Corey Podolsky, Evan Schnittman, and Shaun Wolfe.

Introduction

There is no mistaking the extent to which the Internet has changed nearly every aspect of our lives: how we shop, how we work, how we find a potential mate, how we relate to each other as a global community. The Internet has enabled someone in Seattle, Washington, to talk to someone in Beijing, China, with the click of a mouse—and to discover that they have more in common than was otherwise thought. It is truly an amazing force that has both its advantages and its drawbacks.

One of the more amazing things about the Internet—and a theme that is stressed repeatedly throughout this book—is the extent to which the Internet, and its related technologies, are changing and evolving. What started out as a simple network among a few college campuses now literally connects the world. And the Internet has given rise to a whole new area in which to establish a career and make a living. Some of these are long-established professions, like sales and advertising, and the Internet has enabled these people to reach potential clients in ways never before imagined. Other professions, like Webmaster, Web site consultant, and multimedia professional, never would have come about were it not for the Internet.

As Chapter 1 explains, the idea for this remarkable network was born in the mind of Tim Berners-Lee, a man who is still active in making sure that the Internet remains true to his original vision. Contrary to popular belief, the Internet is not a place of lawlessness where anyone can do anything they want. There are organizations that establish and maintain standards for the Internet, standards in which Berners-Lee firmly believes. Chapter 1 also provides a detailed overview of the history of the Internet. By understanding how the Internet came about and the forces that shaped it, one can get a better grasp on where the future of the Internet lies.

Chapter 2 builds on the foundation established in Chapter 1 and examines the state of the industry. It provides information on salaries and employment trends, how the Internet has changed the face of advertising, who "regulates" the Internet, and more. Profiles of industry-leading companies are provided, as are summaries of important conferences and tradeshows where emerging trends can be viewed firsthand. These two chapters also provide insightful interviews with professionals who know this industry inside-out.

These people offer the benefit of their experience, with information on possible opportunities, where the "hot" areas are, and what makes the most "business sense."

Chapter 3 describes in detail the various jobs and positions one may find in the Internet industry. And there are many more than you might have originally thought. When a lot of people think of "Internet-related" jobs, they may think of programmers or die-hard eBay sellers—people running a Web site and somehow making money off it. These jobs are certainly included in this chapter (in fact, there is an extensive section aimed specifically at Internet entrepreneurs), but the umbrella of "Internet jobs" is large, encompassing a wide range of professions, from writers and illustrators to programmers and developers, marketers and advertisers to teachers and consultants. Practically any job these days can be translated to the Internet. This chapter also shows where certain fields overlap so that those interested in moving up the career ladder will understand how to do so in a way that makes the most sense in light of their career goals.

Now that you have your foot in the door, Chapter 4 offers specific tips on how to establish a professional reputation—whether you work at home in your pajamas or in a large corporation. And while this book assumes that readers already have an Internet-related job, it does not assume that the job a person has now is the job that he or she will always have. Thus, this chapter also offers tips on job hunting and how to conduct a successful interview. Learn firsthand from a longtime professional in this field the quickest things that can make or break a professional reputation and what it takes to make it.

The Internet has spawned a language all its own—a lot of it consisting of shorthand spellings, weird acronyms, and words that sound like gibberish. In order to make certain that readers are up to speed from day one, Chapter 5 provides an extensive, in-depth glossary of industry jargon, defining and explaining key concepts and phrases so that even if a person is new to the industry, they will not sound like it.

This book aims to be complete as possible in limited space. By necessity, some areas, while fascinating, just cannot be explored in this book or can only be touched on briefly. Therefore, Chapter 6 is designed to round out the other chapters in this book. It contains a lengthy guide to all sorts of resources so that especially motivated career launchers can learn more. There are books, periodicals, Web sites, and training programs, any of which can help you manage your career successfully and get the most out of it.

Throughout each chapter, you will find the following boxed items, which contain information that supplements the text:

→ **Best Practices:** These will tell you how to improve your efficiency and performance in the workplace. Some are aimed at the Internet industry in general; others apply to specific areas, such as how to ensure that office politics do not become a problem or how to advertise successfully on the Internet.

→ **Everyone Knows:** These items provide essential information that everyone in the Internet arena should know. Whether you are a computer programmer, technical writer, or a Web consultant, this information is crucial. Not knowing these things might even cost you a job!

→ **Fast Facts:** On the other hand, if you want to impress someone in your next interview (or even win a game of Trivial Pursuit), you might toss out one of these handy tidbits of information. These items provide fun, useful bits of information that, while not necessary knowledge, may make you look good.

→ **Keeping in Touch:** The Internet has undoubtedly changed the forms in which we communicate. Yet, the ways in which we communicate—in person or across the globe—have not really changed. Clear communication is still as essentially now as ever. These items will provide tips for effective business communication—through e-mail, on the phone, and in person—and include pointers on maintaining professionalism at all times. Effective networking tips are also included.

→ **On the Cutting Edge:** These items discuss emerging trends and state-of-the-art technology in this industry. You may find these items helpful when considering a specialty or looking toward the future of your career.

→ **Problem Solving:** While this book cannot possibly cover every contingency, it can describe common, hypothetical problems often encountered by people in this industry and offer possible solutions. Some are relevant to those working in a corporation; others are more fitting for the sole Internet entrepreneur.

→ **Professional Ethics:** Just as professionalism is important—regardless of the career you are in or how lax your boss is (even if you are your own boss!)—so are strong ethics. These items describe an ethical dilemma and its successful resolution, with an emphasis on how ethical conduct can help build a strong career.

The Internet is truly an amazing phenomenon. It is not hyperbole to say that modern human history can be divided into "life before the Internet" and "life after the Internet," as it can with respect to other great milestones. Congratulations on launching a career in this exciting, ever-changing field! Where you go from here is completely up to you.

Chapter 1

Industry History

Most of the more than 1.5 billion people who use the Internet every day probably do not give the technology behind it a second thought. Many might know that the Internet is really shorthand for a big collection of connections—millions of computers linked to each other through a galaxy of networks. Others might think of the Internet as just "the World Wide Web," that daily destination where we shop, talk, work, study, learn, and play.

Online or offline, there is so much more to the story of the Internet. It is not a long history as measured in years (barely 40), but the impact of the Internet has been unprecedented in its scale and scope. The Internet is such a unique chapter in human history that anyone looking to make the most out of a career in this field will need to understand it inside and out.

This chapter describes in detail the history of the Internet, from its relatively modest origins to the revolutionary changes it has made in every corner of people's lives. Along the way, this chapter will explain the who, what, when, why, and how of the Internet's development. It will detail the technological triumphs and exciting new possibilities so that people embarking on an Internet-based career will understand how the Internet's past has shaped its present, and what that suggests about its future. This understanding will give insight on how to gain success in this exciting and relatively new field.

The Beginnings

In a way, the origins of the Internet can be traced to *Sputnik*. In October 1957, the Soviet Union launched *Sputnik*, the first satellite. This milestone came in the middle of a tense Cold War, and caused the United States to scramble to achieve and maintain a technological and scientific advantage over the Soviet Union. One important move was the Department of Defense's creation of the Advanced Research Projects Agency, or ARPA, in 1958. ARPA created the Information Processing Technology Office (IPTO). IPTO's task was to develop a strong, secure network linking large computers. These computers were similar to the Atanasoff Berry Computer (ABC), designed by John Atanasoff. A professor from Iowa State College, Atanasoff first conceived of the device in 1930. His design consisted of a rotating drum on which 1,600 capacitors (pairs of conductors separated by a nonconducting substance) were placed in 32 rows. Each capacitor could be charged positively, indicating a 1, or negatively, indicating a 0. This is called the binary principle, and today's computers still operate in this way. According to Mike Hally, the author of *Electronic Brains: Stories from the Dawn of the Computer Age*, the ABC was "as big as a fridge, weighed a third of a ton, and used more than 300 tubes . . . and it took 15 seconds to complete an arithmetic calculation."

By the 1950s, the idea of the "personal" computer was starting to take form, and by the 1960s, there were significant improvements to the computer's user interface. Both private and government-funded research projects were everywhere. In addition to ARPA, Massachusetts Institute of Technology (MIT), IPTO, Dartmouth College, and Stanford Research Institute had similar projects in the works. These projects led to the development of the mouse, computer networks, the BASIC programming language (BASIC stands for Beginner's All-purpose Symbolic Instruction Code), and the concept of time sharing, among other things. (Time sharing, in this context, refers to sharing computer resources through multitasking.)

In July 1961, Leonard Kleinrock, a computer scientist at MIT, published the first paper on packet-switching theory. Kleinrock believed that packets—units of information transmitted in their entirety from one device to another on a network—rather than circuits were the key to computer networking. The other key step was to make the computers "talk" to each other. A small experiment in which a computer in Massachusetts was connected to one in California with a low-speed dial-up telephone line—creating the first wide-area computer network, albeit a small one—proved that time-shared computers could work well together. They could run programs and retrieve data on the remote computer, but the circuit-switched telephone system (the system in use back then) was inadequate for the job. The need for packet switching was confirmed.

In August 1962, J. C. R. Licklider, another computer scientist at MIT, wrote a series of memos detailing a globally interconnected set of computers through which everyone could quickly access data and programs from any site. Always forward-thinking, Licklider recognized several hurdles that would need to be overcome before his vision of a "mechanically extended man" could be realized. Paul Ceruzzi, the author of *The History of Modern Computing*, writes: "Some [technical hurdles] involved hardware limits, which existing trends in computer circuits would soon overcome. [Others involved] redefining the notions of programming and data storage as they were then practiced." Thus, the idea of the Internet was beginning to germinate and take form.

In 1969, packet switching enabled computers at UCLA to talk to computers at the University of Utah, the University of California–Santa Barbara, and other sites. These were the first nodes of what would become a larger computer network of universities, laboratories, and government agencies in ARPANET. In 1970, ARPANET went coast-to-coast, connecting BBN Technologies in Cambridge, Massachusetts, to the network.

BBN, known originally as Bolt, Beranek, and Newman, tells the story of their role in origins of the Internet as follows. In 1968, the company responded to a request for quotation (RFQ) from ARPA to build a network of four interface message processors (IMPs). They were awarded the contract in January 1969. The software team worked practically nonstop on the project, figuring out how to automatically pull in packets, route them, and send them on their way while simultaneously updating itself several times per second. The hardware team was working just as hard, designing the high-speed input/output (I/O) devices that would be needed to make the software work as desired.

Two weeks before the UCLA installation deadline, a huge hurdle still needed to be overcome: the network crashed frequently at random intervals. A likely solution was finally hit upon, but there was no time to test it. The network machines were shipped out, and the teams at BBN waited with bated breath.

At UCLA, the team attached the cables, powered up the IMP, and crossed their fingers. Instantly, the machine resumed activities begun in Cambridge. When the network ran for a few days without crashing the team was ecstatic. On October 1, 1969, a second IMP arrived at the Stanford Research Institute and the first characters were transmitted over the new network. The ARPANET was born. When IMPs number three and four were installed at University of California–Santa Barbara, and the University of Utah, IMP installations were beginning to seem routine and there was little outside interest in the project. The network quietly expanded to 13 sites by January 1971 and to 23 sites by April 1972.

Through the 1970s, the pace of invention quickened. Transmission protocols improved, standards were set, network communication went global, and the first real e-mail programs were developed. The first e-mail program was developed in the early 1970s. In late 1971, Ray Tomlinson was working on a small team at BBN Technologies developing the TENEX operating system, using local e-mail programs called SNDMSG and READMAIL. Tomlinson developed the first ARPANET e-mail application when he updated SNDMSG by adding a program called CPYNET capable of copying files over the network, and informed his colleagues by sending them an e-mail using the new program with instructions on how to use it.

According to Tomlinson, to extend the addressing to the network, he chose the @ symbol to combine the user and host names, creating the naturally meaningful notation (user@host) that is the standard for e-mail addressing today. These early programs had simple functionality and were command-line driven, but they established the basic transactional model that still defines the technology: e-mail gets sent to a person's inbox.

California scientists Bob Braden, Vinton Cerf, Bob Kahn, John Postel, and others in the Networking Group developed what would become the backbone of the Internet—the protocol called TCP/IP, or Transmission Control Protocol-Internet Protocol, which makes it possible to build and move packets of data from one computer to another.

Around 1974 the word *Internet* was coined as shorthand for "internetworking." It is important to remember that until the commercialization of the Internet in the 1980s and especially the 1990s, the Internet was seen not as an e-mail highway between people (to say nothing of a new way of doing business), but as a way for scientists to do high-level computing through time-sharing over a network. The

Internet linked research institutions, and offered scientists and other researchers a way to do massive calculations by accessing the power of another computer through secure, standards-based systems. This, in turn, meant that the cost of producing computer capabilities was reduced, individuals and companies could use a computer without incurring the cost to actually own one, and the development of new interactive applications was spurned on.

During the 1970s and 1980s, the Internet continued to be built—experiment by experiment, local network by local network—at sites around the world. The early and mid-1970s were especially alive with invention. In labs from Los Angeles to London, scientists were developing the technologies, protocols, and systems that would transform the world of communication.

By 1975, the first full-scale e-mail management program, MSG, was ready to help users compose, reply to, forward, and file their messages. The same year, the first ARPANET mailing list appeared. Its most popular list was one devoted to science fiction, which might come as no surprise. By 1976, Queen Elizabeth II was using e-mail.

Meanwhile, network architecture was being dramatically improved. In 1970, the first host-to-host protocol, NCP, appeared, followed in the next year by the first Terminal Interface Processor (TIP), finally allowing direct dial-ups to the network. The first FTP, or file transfer protocol, specification was also released. Two years later, Robert Kahn and Vinton Cerf described the first Internet working protocol, TCP, in a paper—and start working on it. TCP was first conceived by the Department of Defense for communication between computers. It is the de facto standard for data transmission over networks, including the Internet. In 1972, Lawrence Roberts published a theory of radio packet transmissions that would become the foundation of today's WiFi standard. In 1977, the new Internet TCP protocols were used to link three networks—ARPANET, SF Bay Packet radio Net, and Atlantic SATNET (a satellite network).

Technological advances were mirrored by new uses, as networks got larger and more connected to each other. In 1974, America's first licensed public data network opened. Called Telnet and based on the X.25 transmission standard, it was founded by ARPA's Larry Roberts and financed by BBN, with a goal of making ARPANET's technology public. Originally defined by the International Telegraph and Telephone Consultative Committee, the X.25 protocol is a standard suite for packet-switched wide area network (WAN) communication. An X.25 WAN consists of packet-switching exchange (PSE) nodes as the networking hardware, and leased lines, plain old telephone service (POTS) connections, or ISDN connections as physical links. This family of protocols was used primarily during the 1980s by telecommunications companies and in financial transaction systems such as automated teller machines. Today, X.25 has been almost completely replaced by less complex protocols—in particular, the Internet Protocol (IP)—although some telephone operators offer X.25-based communication via the signaling (D) channel of ISDN lines.

AT&T turned down an offer for the technology in the late 1970s, claiming it had no future! Meanwhile, Telnet became the first commercial network using the basic packet-switching technology that has made the Internet possible. Telnet was sold to GTE in 1979 and later bought by Sprint, where it became one of the networks that make up today's Internet.

Piece by piece, these and other advances began to show the potential of the Internet. What began as a focused research program driven by military and national security needs started to spool out—like the old Teletype paper it would eventually make obsolete. As scientists continued their work building protocols and systems, they enabled networks to grow and gather around the world.

In 1983, the TCP/IP suite became the standard protocol for ARPANET, and would soon become the glue that bound the different systems to a single standard of data transmission. The Domain Name System (DNS) was established in 1984 and would later be called "the mother of all systems." DNS translates a host's Internet Protocol (IP) numbers to domain names—creating the world's largest database of connected addresses. This allowed people to use meaningful URLs and e-mail addresses without having to know how the computer would actually locate them. Over the next few years, Internet protocols were improved and standardized, and implemented more broadly.

As a result of DNS, network-to-network communication became easier, and networks started proliferating, growing from 1,000 hosts in 1984 to 10,000 in 1987 and 100,000 in 1989. The Internet community at this stage still largely comprised scientific research centers at universities, in the government, and in private labs. The National Science Foundation (NSF) established NSFNET in 1984, with five supercomputing university centers at Princeton, the University of Pittsburgh, Cornell, the University of Illinois at Urbana-Champaign, and the University of California–San Diego, expanding the reach of these networks.

Outside academia, local public-interest networks, or Freenets, in cities like Cleveland and San Francisco provided conferencing, data transfer, and other connections to activist groups. Tom Truscott and Jim Ellis, graduate students at Duke University, conceived the idea in of Usenet in 1979. Users read and posted public messages (called articles or posts, and collectively termed *news*) to one or more categories, known as newsgroups. After its public unveiling in 1980, Usenet groups exploded in number thanks to the power of TCP/IP standards. More and more countries were connecting to the networks.

With close to 1 million hosts by this point, cyberspace was rich in data, from simple e-mail messages to complicated files supporting scientific research. Before the World Wide Web, these files were not easy to reach, search, or send. The most common method of storage and retrieval, File Transfer Protocol (FTP), offered a way to exchange files, but many important files and archives were still hidden on many small servers scattered across many different hosts, with no way for users to search for files. A search engine called Archie was developed in 1990 at McGill University in Montreal, and was the first of a number of tools that helped navigate the ever-growing universe of data. It combed and indexed FTP sites across the Internet. Two other search engines—Veronica (developed in 1992 by Steven Foster and Fred Barrie at the University of Nevada–Reno) and Jughead (developed by Rhett Jones in 1993 at the University of Utah)— helped students, scholars, and scientists search and retrieve archived information. It was not always easy or pretty, but it worked.

By 1990, ARPANET had been decommissioned and various segments transferred to other entities, such as NSFNET and the Department of Defense, and the Internet had begun to expand beyond its original communities in education, research, and defense. After MCI Mail and CompuServe got connected to the network, other commercial services followed, including OnTyme and Telemail. The first three commercial Internet Service Providers (ISPs) were also created (UUNET, PSINet and CERFNET), and a variety of other local networks, including BITNET and Usenet, both commercial and educational, got connected to the Internet. The increasing availability of routers—electronic devices used to connect two or more computers or other electronic devices to each other, and usually to the Internet, by wire or radio signals (from companies such as Cisco Systems); the rapid spread of Ethernet technologies (a means of connecting local computer networks); and the implementation of TCP/IP suites, helped make the creation of local and wide area networks ever more possible. A local area network (LAN) is a group of computers and other devices dispersed over a relatively small area and connected by a link that enables devices and computers to communicate with one another. By way of contrast, a wide area network (WAN) connects geographically separated areas.

Fast Facts

Worldwide Percentages

There are 1.6 billion Internet users worldwide—24 percent of all people. This number has grown 344 percent since 2000. China has the most users, with 278 million, although this is only 22.4 percent of their population. The number of users has grown 1,224 percent since 2000. China accounts for almost 18 percent of the world's Internet users. The United States has the second most users, with 220 million, which is 73 percent of the population. The number of users has grown 130 percent since 2000.

The World Wide Web: Everything Changes

In Switzerland, at the European Organization for Nuclear Research (CERN), a young physicist named Tim Berners-Lee was confronting a problem: He wanted to present scientific data to physicists around the world who shared neither hardware nor software. Berners-Lee had written a proposal for "a large hypertext database with typed links." Working on a new NeXT workstation (a Steve Jobs innovation), he and his colleagues showed how information could be transferred easily by joining hypertext—the now-familiar "point and click" method of navigating among linked documents—to the Internet.

In 1991, the National Science Foundation formally opened the Internet backbone to commercial use, lifting a 20-year ban on using the Internet for this purpose. Something new would be waiting. By the end of the year, Berners-Lee had created everything necessary for a viable World Wide Web, including hypertext transfer protocol (HTTP), the first HTTP server software, the first Web browser, the World Wide Web, and the first Web pages.

Berners-Lee's breakthrough came at what, looking back, was an almost perfect time. The 1980s had been feverish with innovation and growth, and healthy competition had brought computing to more and more users. IBM, Apple, Tandy, Compaq, NeXT, Digital, and other companies fought for market share. The mouse was invented in 1984, the first pocket and personal digital devices appeared, and laptops became more common. By the late 1980s, personal and workstation computers were a fact of everyday life, even if by today's standards, machines were heavy, slow, and expensive. (The Macintosh Portable of 1989 weighed 16 pounds and cost $7,300—and did not have much in the way of memory—only 64 KB!)

At the close of 1990, there were 92 million personal computers in American homes, or 1 in 4 homes; what's more, 17 percent had a modem attached to their PCs. The early Internet was a noisy, busy place—navigable only through clumsy search tools like Archie, Jughead, and Veronica—but there was an active community of scientists, engineers, students, and businesspeople using it. Scholars researched huge text archives; businesses sent invoices, bills, and did stock transfers via EDI, or electronic data interchange; thousands of other users shared ideas and opinions in Usenet groups and new virtual communities. FidoNet, BITNET, and other local networks now linked millions of computers.

The Internet was largely in place, its protocols able to link operating systems and local networks into one universal, seamless world of communication. Until 1993, the Internet remained a limited, if powerful tool—you could use it to send a message, move a text file, or search an archive, but there was a disconnect between the big backbone of the Internet and the growing uses of personal computing. By 1992, there were 1 million Internet hosts, but fewer than 100 sites (hosts are what enable access to Web sites). Sales of personal computers were exploding—10 million copies of Windows 3.0 and more than 25 million personal computers were shipped in 1992 alone.

Berners-Lee made the gap between the Internet and the World Wide Web clear in an interview in the 1990s. "The Web is an abstract (imaginary) space of information," he said. "On the Net, you find computers—on the Web, you find documents, sounds, video information. On the Net, the connections are cables between computers; on the Web, connections are hypertext links. The Web exists because of programs that communicate between computers on the Net. The Web could not be without the Net. The Web made the Net useful because people are really interested in information (not to mention knowledge and wisdom!) and do not really want to have know about computers and cables."

It took more than 30 years to develop the technology, standards, and protocols for the Internet—for sending and receiving and accessing data easily from network to network. It was not until 1993 that the Internet's fullest potential could be realized—when the Internet was finally given a public face—in the form of a graphical interface. This graphic interface was a new browser called Mosaic, and it changed everything.

While Berners-Lee had developed a graphical interface for the Web in 1991, the program ran only on his NeXT desktop. By Berners-Lee's design, all of his World Wide Web software was available for free on the Internet; soon, other programmers started to join the quest to create a user-friendly, graphic interface. One of these pioneers was a student at the University of Illinois named Marc Andreessen, who helped develop the Mosaic browser for the National Center for Supercomputing Application. Along with James Clark, former Stanford professor and chairman of the Silicon Graphics, Inc., he formed the Mosaic Communications Corporation, and introduced Mosaic in 1993. In 1994, Mosaic changed its name to Netscape Navigation Communications, and, building on some original Mosaic code, developed the leading browser of the day.

The impact of the Mosaic program, which portrayed text and graphics together on the screen for the first time, was felt immediately. In *Wired* magazine, Gary Wolfe noted, "Do not look now, but Prodigy, AOL, and CompuServe are all suddenly obsolete—and Mosaic is well on its way to becoming the world's standard interface that allows users to travel through the world of electronic information using a point-and-click interface [and] load their own documents onto the Net, including color photos, sound bites, video clips, and hypertext 'links' to other documents . . . Mosaic has incited a rush of excitement and commercial energy unprecedented in the history of the Net."

Andreessen and his team realized the mass appeal of the Internet, and by turning a browser meant for the institutional world served by the Unix platform into a multiplatform gift for the millions of personal computers running on Windows, he put the Internet into everyone's hands. This was a classic chapter in the growth of the Internet: Innovation seeded by public funds and driven by a vision of democratic access to information.

Other browsers soon entered the marketplace, including Cello, Arena, and Lynx. Mosaic, now called Netscape, soon became the world's standard interface. However, Netscape was quickly met with competition from other browsers, including IBM's Web Explorer. Netscape went public in 1995, but would soon face its fiercest competition from Microsoft's Internet Explorer in what would later be called the "browser wars" of the 1990s. It was a battle Netscape would lose, and by the end of the decade, Netscape could not compete with the larger Microsoft, which invested heavily in Explorer, and bundled it as a free feature it with its Windows suite. Netscape was bought by AOL in 1998, but eventually lost its market share to Explorer. By 2003, Explorer held 96 percent of the browser market. Time Warner (formerly AOL Time Warner) formally disbanded Netscape in 2003. The Netscape 7.2 Web browser (developed in-house rather than with Netscape staff) was released by AOL on August 18, 2004.

But Netscape did not completely disappear. Back in 1998, Netscape had started what was to become the Mozilla Foundation in order to build a competitive browser using the open-source software model. (Open-source refers to the free exchange and collaboration of developers and producers.) Netscape would be gone, but the browser eventually evolved into Firefox, released in 2004 by The Mozilla Corporation, a taxable offshoot of the Mozilla Foundation. (Today the Mozilla Corporation is a $66 million company.) Firefox built on open-source software contributed by a community of programmers. As of 2009, Firefox claimed about 22 percent of browser usage, a number that continues to grow. Other browsers of the early twenty-first century include Apple's Safari, with less than 10 percent of the market, and smaller, specialized browsers like Opera, which is used by a large chunk of the mobile phone market. In February 2009, Internet Explorer's share of the browser market was 69.23 percent; by December 2009, it had fallen to 62.69 percent.

The browser story—the Netscape story, in short—was a crucial turning point in Internet history. "Even as late as 1995, the Net was populated by early adopters, defense contractors, techies, and academics," Marc Andreessen told *Wired* a decade later. "It was completely unclear whether it would spread beyond that to consumers and business users. People still thought interactive TV would rule the world."

By 1995, close to half of Americans said they had heard of something called "the World Wide Web." In the same year, Amazon.com went live, and AltaVista, the first major search engine, indexed 10 million pages. By 1995, you could order from Pizza Hut on your browser. The age of the Web was here, and it brought with it an entirely new economy.

Web 1.0: Commerce, Culture, and Change

Until 1991, commerce on the Internet was expressly forbidden by the National Science Foundation, which ran the Internet's principal backbone. Even after NSF opened the pipeline to commerce, many still doubted that the Internet would ever be a way to run a sustainable business—much less, realize a profit. "I'm not sure how you'd make money out of it," a telecom executive said in 1994.

Before the Netscape breakout, the Internet was thought to be a boring business tool. At its most adventurous, it was thought that the Internet would be a kind of supersized television, with 5,000 channels of expensive content and varieties of virtual reality provided

Everyone
Knows

ROM vs. RAM

People often use the term "memory" when discussing their computer's hard drive. However, this is actually an incomplete (albeit common) use of the term. RAM (random access memory) is where programs that are currently being used by the processor to run the program are held. This "cache" is cleared when you shut down the computer. ROM (read only memory) is where all programs on your computer are stored until you need them. This is the hard drive; items stored here stay here until you remove them.

David Patterson, author of *Computer Organization and Design*, uses a great analogy to explain how this works: Think of the hard drive (ROM) as a file cabinet. It contains all of the programs your computer needs to operate. RAM can be thought of as a desktop (an actual desktop, not the virtual "desktop" on your computer!). When you open a program you want to work on, it is like taking a file from the file cabinet and moving it to your desktop. When you are done working on the program, you put the file back into the file cabinet for long-term storage. By that analogy, if you have a system crash or a power failure while working on something on the desktop, it is as if a window opens and a strong breeze blows everything off the desk before you can put it away.

by the old media and paid for by largely passive consumers. Most people, it seemed, could not see what the Internet would become, or what it would change. But something was taking hold. The numbers tell the tale: The 130 Web sites counted in 1993 blossomed twenty-fold to 2,800 the following year, and to 230,000 in 1996. The 21,000 domains registered in 1993 grew to 240,000 by 1996. The 1.3 million hosts, or machine addresses, of 1993 became 9.5 million in 1996. And this was only the beginning. Today, Google takes in billions of searches every month, and the number of Web pages on the Internet is measured in the hundreds of billions.

After Netscape, the Internet became all about the World Wide Web, even as e-mail, file transfers, and other operations continued to hum through cables and phone lines. Households and business got connected, and everything, it seemed, had its own Web page and domain name.

At first the Web was largely a new vehicle for displaying information, or for promoting an enterprise. Largely static, these mid-nineties sites provided instant access to everything from a college course catalog, to a guide to a hospital's services, to promotional pages describing consumer products. Many firms thought of Web sites as multimedia 800 numbers, but little more. Others were quick to see that the Web's ability to deliver hyperlinked data offered enormous commercial opportunities, especially in key sectors such as entertainment or publishing. The Web experience itself would shape new businesses—provided entrepreneurs could predict what users would want to pay for. The answers were not always easy to come by.

Almost as soon as Netscape opened the Web to the public, investors and entrepreneurs started launching thousands of new ventures to take advantage of the Internet. During the boom that took place from 1998 to 2001, an estimated 6,000 firms raised almost $100 billion in venture capital. More than 400 IPOs, or initial public offerings, were made during the boom years. Millionaires and billionaires were made in the trading of technology stocks. It seemed not to matter than many of the new Internet ventures kept losing money, nor that many seemed to have no plan for making money in the future. "Burn rates"—or the speed with which these ventures used up investor capital—were about the only financial data anyone watched. The market was so volatile that Alan Greenspan, then chairman of the Federal Reserve, warned of the dangers of "irrational exuberance"— that is, investing in the promises and hopes for what the Internet would bring rather than on what was actually being produced.

In the middle of 2000, the NASDAQ index of technology stocks collapsed, and boom became bust: Stocks crashed, thousands of people lost jobs, and firms went bankrupt or downsized before disappearing entirely. It is estimated that between 2000 and 2002, technology stocks lost $12 trillion in market value. While there were other conditions in play, one reason for the bust was the race for market share—as new ventures spent investor capital to find and hold customers, or to build expensive infrastructure—without a solid business plan.

Although many small, lean dot-coms survived, there were garish failures like Boo.com, a fashion retailer that spent $188 million in six months before going bankrupt in 2000; or Webvan.com, an online grocer that promised deliveries in 30 minutes, which went bankrupt in 2001."Get large or get lost" was the mantra, but only a few ventures were carefully managed enough to make it work. Those that have survived include Internet Movie Database (bought by Amazon in 1998), PayPal (bought by eBay in 2002), and YouTube (bought by Google in 2006).

The Internet era saw a migration of traditional businesses to the Web as well as the establishment of startups that could not exist without it. In the business-to-businesses sector, Web technologies and practices offered new efficiencies. This was particularly true of B2B services. Here, the Web increased efficiencies, lowered costs, and added enormous user value to databases, directories, and archives of highly specialized and hard to get information that was strategically valued because it was centrally located and easily searched.

LexisNexis provides an excellent example of the benefits of migrating to the Web. This provider of data offers full text access to legal, government, and media documents on a subscription basis to colleges, universities, law firms, corporations, and other clients. It has been delivering content electronically since the 1970s, and expanded its reach on the Web to 80 million worldwide users. Other traditional business-to-business retailers benefited by using the Web as an easy way to mount a visually rich, easy-to-explore product catalog, coupled to online ordering, invoicing, and customer relations and support. These include suppliers and wholesalers in almost every industry.

Not every start-up failed, of course, and even with the dot-com bust, U.S. online retail revenues jumped from $24 to $34 billion during the early years of the twenty-first century, exploding to $130 billion in 2006. The number of Americans who were online grew

INTERVIEW

Technological Changes Lead to Cultural Changes

Michael Jensen
Director of Strategic Web Communications,
The National Academies, Washington, D.C.

How has the Internet changed the way you do business?
The onset—one might even say "onslaught"—of the Web has had predictable as well as unanticipated consequences on our culture, our businesses, even our personal relationships. In the 1990s, we publishers were still talking about whether to initiate "Web departments" within our businesses, while reality quietly trumped us: The Web became integral to marketing, communications, promotion, sales, even production. While there still are IT departments that handle the plumbing of our digital infrastructure, the notion of having a separate "Web department" went the way of the fax, or the telephone—it became so interwoven a function, it was counterproductive to centralize.

What new technologies or trends have you noticed or do you anticipate?
The underlying technologies of the Web continue to change (from HTML to XHTML to XML and AJAX), but for most purposes, the technology hardly matters. It is really about communications, presentation, and brand promotion. The specific technologies may be useful to understand, but is no more required than knowing the database structure underlying an order fulfillment system. What matters more is understanding what expectations our audiences (and we ourselves) have, and how to respond to those expectations.

How can success best be measured in the Internet age?
Whether a publisher, a widget maker, a consultancy, or a stockbroker, the same questions remain: What do my customers expect, and how can I shine within that environment? If a Facebook fan page is expected, or a Twitter feed, or a free sample chapter, or a video explanation, then it is our job to provide that to our customers.

Thankfully, the tools for producing this stuff have become simpler, cheaper, and faster; a great deal of the work can be done in-house to keep costs down. In the end, it is not about knowing the ins and outs of technology, but the ins and outs of our culture, as it changes its expectations about the application of our communications technologies.

even faster—from 125 million (44 percent of the population) in 2000 to 210 million (71 percent) in 2006. As high-speed connectivity became cheaper and easier to get, browsers and search engines got more robust, and Web sites became less costly (and less complicated) to develop. By 2000, almost every company and public institution had a Web presence—it has been estimated that there were 7 million unique sites on the Web in 2000.

After the bust, businesses that did not flame out still found that there were no simple keys to success in the digital economy. Portals, for example, give users a branded, one-stop source for links to other sites; they also consolidate and organize content from across the Web (Yahoo! MSN, AOL). These would seem to be cannot-miss ideas. But discovering the commercial values of portals proved to be difficult, and it still remains unclear which portal-based features users are willing to pay for.

The stories of companies that used the Web to engineer success provide insights into the distinctive nature of the digital economy. It may have taken years for these ventures to show a profit, but their journeys to success show brilliantly how the Internet has reshaped the way we live. Their stories also suggest what might happen next with Web 2.0 and Web 3.0. Southwest Airlines offers an excellent case study of a traditional company that used the innovative technology and Internet to streamline costs, increase customer loyalty and satisfaction, and grow its market share. It was the first airline to establish an Internet home page. In 2008, 78 percent of all Southwest passengers booked their travel online at Southwest.com. Seven million people subscribe to the airline's weekly e-mail notification service, and 66 percent of Fortune 500 companies are enrolled in Southwest's free online tool for managing business travel. Among airline Web sites, the site is the largest in number of unique visits, and always among the largest in online revenue. The airline itself, known for lean management, low cost, and consistent quality, has had more than 30 years of profitability. Its pioneering Web site has played a big role in its success.

Amazon.com is perhaps the leading example of an Internet venture that transformed traditional retailing, and, in the process, invented new models of e-commerce. Amazon began on the Web in 1995, when its founder, Jeff Bezos, decided that books—as well as videos, compact discs, and computer software and hardware—would work best in his Internet store. Amazon.com opened with a searchable inventory of more than one million titles—only 2,000 of which Amazon actually stocked. Instead, orders were filled from traditional wholesalers and publishers. Offering an unmatched range of titles, easy searching, a customer-friendly site, rock-solid security, and quick service, Amazon grew quickly. In 1997, it became the first Internet retailer to have more than one million customers. Amazon's 1997 IPO allowed Bezos to build from within, enhancing an already successful Web site and adding an East Coast distribution center.

Amazon's growth came from many sources: a diversity of product offerings—from books, software, and music to shirts, shoes, and sporting goods—and profitable third-party advertising and promotion arrangements with thousands of associates. The company fought to grow market share in many sectors, building enormous customer databases. It survived the bust of 2000 by cutting costs and expanding sales volume by introducing discounts. The next year, with sales over $3 billion, it turned a $5 million profit.

Amazon's story is not just one of a big box retailer that happens to be online and that happens to offer unmatched selection, convenience, and savings. Its story is important not for what—or how well—it sells goods, or how right it has been in its technology strategy. Its success has come from its ability to recognize the importance of connecting with people not only as shoppers or names on a mailing list but as active, involved participants in creating and re-creating the business with every click-through and every purchase. Amazon's famous gallery of user features—recommendations, reviews, personalized profiles, customized notifications, and more—built loyalty and traffic. By 2008, the Amazon model would echo a new stage for the Internet. It would also produce sales of $8.9 billion.

Google represents a best case of a venture that could not exist before the Internet. It is neither a business-to-business service provider nor vendor, nor a retailer. Its features are free for anyone to use. How did it become a company with 22,000 employees and $22 billion in revenues in little more than decade?

Sergey Brin and Larry Page started Google as a search engine in their Stanford University dorm room in the mid-1990s, and turned a $100,000 investment from a founder of Sun Microsystems into what many consider the most powerful brand in the world. Google's inventive, easy-to-use search engine—which get good results by ranking pages based on the number of links they had to other pages—consistently delivered what users were looking for. Searches were fast, free, and uncluttered. Google grew quickly between 2005 and 2008, largely through partnerships (for advertising on MySpace and with AOL for video searching), acquisitions (YouTube.com, for example), the development of tools like Gmail and Google Earth, and its current project to digitize and make available for free millions of books in libraries. Google is now as much identified with the content it can offer as with its search engine. It also has created Web applications, such as Google Calendar, Google Docs, and Google Sites. It is the most visited set of sites on the Internet, with 146 billion unique visitors in 2008.

Web 1.0 Begets Web 2.0

By the early years of the twenty-first century, the Internet offered many lessons about adapting to, surviving, and thriving in a digital economy. Observers call this early stage of the Internet Web 1.0. The term does not refer to a particular technology, but rather defines how the Web was used during this period.

Roughly speaking, Web 1.0 refers to a model of a static, hierarchical Web that does not allow users to contribute anything. Web 1.0 applications are usually proprietary. Web 1.0 ventures are not usually built to incorporate, or make any use of, customer profiles, preferences, or behaviors. This was the Web everyone knew before the dot-com bubble burst in 2000. Terry Flew, author of *New Media*, describes the primary differences between Web 1.0 and Web 2.0 as a "move from personal Web sites to blogs and blog site aggregation, from publishing to participation, from Web content as the outcome of large up-front investment to an ongoing and interactive process, and from content management systems to links based on tagging."

Thus, the shift from Web 1.0 to Web 2.0 can be linked to technological refinements, which, according to Dion Hinchcliffe in his article "All We Got Was Web 1.0, When Tim Berners-Lee Actually Gave Us Web 2.0," included such adaptations as "broadband, improved browsers, and Ajax, to the rise of Flash application platforms and the mass development of widgetization, such as Flickr and YouTube badges." Rapid advances in shareware and software, in connectivity and access, continued to revolutionize the Internet. Ever since Netscape opened it all up in 1994, the World Wide Web has not only grown in scope, but also in reach.

As Kevin Kelly noted in *Wired* in 2005, when Netscape took off "suddenly it became clear that ordinary people could create material anyone with a connection could view. The burgeoning online audience no longer needed [an] ABC for content." Kelly stated, "The scope of the Web is hard to fathom. How could we create so much, so fast, so well? The electricity of participation nudges ordinary folks

Best
Practice

Powering Down

To turn on or to turn off–that is the question. And the answer may spark more debate than it seems to warrant. Some people fervently recommend leaving a computer on as long as possible, believing that a computer's components come under the most stress when turned off and on, and so a failure is less likely if the computer is left alone. However, while true in theory (or if computer were turned on and off 50 times an hour, every hour), in reality, today's PCs are built better than this. For those who are still not convinced, the power management features that are standard on all PCs enable users to put the machine in "sleep mode" when not in use and "wake" it up in a matter of seconds.

to invest huge hunks of energy and time into making free encyclo-pedias, creating public tutorials for changing a flat tire, or cataloging the votes in the Senate. One study found that only 40 percent of the Web is commercial. The rest runs on duty or passion."

Kelly was describing a broad shift, from the top-down, mass-market model of the Web to something closer to its original spirit of openness, creativity, and collaboration. Embedded into such sites as Amazon, YouTube, and eBay, the flavors of Web 2.0 include a user's ability to make changes to the site—whether it is a product review or recommendation, or, in the case of Firefox, a chance to contribute new code to its open-source programs.

In Web 2.0, pages are used to connect people to people in com-munities of all kinds. In Web 2.0, sharing content is quick, easy, free, and always an assumed option—the Web bookmarking site Delicious makes it simple to share one's favorite sites with anyone, and to see what others have chosen. At the encyclopedia site Wiki-pedia, 75,000 contributors have given 10 million articles to a site visited by 684 million users a year.

Web 2.0 browsing can be customized, through RSS feeds and other programs that notify users about something they might want to read, see, or listen to. RSS formats are specified using XML (eXtensible Markup Language), a generic specification for the creation of data formats. Although RSS formats were in place as early as March 1999, it was between 2005 and 2006 when RSS gained widespread use. Web 2.0 expands our reach beyond the computer itself, as wireless technology puts the Web onto mobile phones and other devices. It also means that one medium can migrate to another, so that television becomes a streamed experience online. Hulu.com, launched in 2008 by NBC, Fox, and Disney, lets users watch thousands of episodes of programs from NBC, Fox, and other sources for free. It is supported by online commercials, and users can embed it on their own pages as well as access videos on demand.

It is too early to know whether Hulu will create a larger storm that might cause the cable television industry to crash, but Hulu can be seen as a way for big media to keep control of content when viewers were consuming more and more video online—mostly for free. It is no surprise that Google has added advertising links to clips on YouTube, and the rumblings of Web 2.0 have provoked many digital players to ask hard questions about commercial viability of new forms, products, and services—lessons learned from Web 1.0.

While much old-fashioned business still gets quietly conducted online, Web 2.0 has generated new targets of invention. In a world where free software helps create millions of blogs, for example, and where millions turn for authoritative information to user-created reference works like Wikipedia, what role will big players face?

Looking Ahead to Web 3.0

It is clear that invention and change on the Internet happens from below—it always has—and that the more the Internet runs on the energy, contributions, and intelligence of its ordinary users, the more powerful it will become. It seems clear that the present and future of the Internet has to assume at least the following: free or low-cost access, ease of use, richness of content, open sourcing, portability, collaboration, and complete interactivity. It is also clear that when consumers and users become creators and change agents, innovation is guaranteed.

There are challenges facing anyone seeking to understand the rules of the Internet game, and they are the natural products of the digital economy. Does all information need to be free? How can some of our most important institutions—newspapers, for example—be transformed into sustainable, monetized digital enterprises when no seems to be willing to pay for online content? What happens to copyright and its protections when Google seeks to digitize and disseminate every book in every library? How do we monitor piracy of music, images, video, and software? Is the Internet ultimately so different from everything that has gone before that no business model can contain it? If the Web becomes the world that defines us, how does that affect issues such as privacy?

These may not even be the questions to ask, as observers see a new Web—Web 3.0—looming out there. An ever more intelligent "semantic" Web will incorporate the social networking features with new technologies that will act as our personal agents in many spheres of life, as the next chapter will explain. It will filter, evaluate, and return individualized content. Application programming interfaces (API) like those found on Facebook will be commonly used to create personalized platforms and programs—and the content created will be shared with circles of friends. A host of new applications, like widgets, might be used to combine mapping, social networking, video, and news feeds into a customized toolkit that could become a common and indispensable device for everyday life.

No one owns the Internet, and it is never off. Speaking on today's and tomorrow's Internet, *Wired*'s Kevin Kelly believes that "the producers are the audience, the act of making is the act of watching, and every link is a point of departure and destination. Online culture is *the* culture." People starting an Internet-based career today are jumping into a world of ceaseless change, confounding unpredictability, and immense promise. The chapters that follow will give a solid grounding in opportunities and challenges this world presents, whether it is a more detailed tour of the Internet landscape or a balanced overview of the social, legal, and even ethical dimensions of the digital economy. As this chapter has shown, it is probably not a good idea to predict too far ahead. If there is a Web 3.0, who knows what it will do, how it will run, what difference it will make in everyone's lives. That is for each person to decide.

A Brief Chronology

1947: The transistor is invented.
1965: The first networking experiment is carried out.
1969: The first two nodes of ARPANET are created.
1971: The first person-to-person e-mail message is sent using the @ sign.

1972: The first basic e-mail programs, SNDMSG and READMAIL, are developed at BBN Technologies.

1974: The term "Internet" is first used to describe a basic TCP/IP network.

1983: Five hundred sixty-two computers are connected to the Internet.

1985: One hundred universities are linked by NSFNET to supercomputing centers.

1988: The first use of the term "search engine" is documented.

1989: Tim Berners-Lee and other scientists propose a World Wide Web.

1991: "Gopher," the first workable user interface for the Internet, is developed at the University of Minnesota.

1992: IBM, MCI, and Microsoft join to create ANS (Advanced Network Services) to build a new national network. Jean Armour Polly, a New York librarian, is credited with first coining the phrase "surfing the Internet" ("surfing the Net" or "surfing the Web" are additional derivations). Polly used the phrase in a 1992 article in the University of Minnesota Wilson Library Bulletin.

1993: The Mosaic browser is developed. There are 130 Web sites. The White House comes online.

1994: The World Wide Web Consortium (W3C) is founded to develop standards for browsers. This is an international community where member organizations, a full-time staff, and the public work together to develop Web standards. Led by Tim Berners-Lee, W3C's mission is to lead the Web to its full potential. Netscape's first browser becomes available, and growing numbers of people start surfing the Web. First Virtual opens as the first cyberbank.

1995: The NSF (National Science Foundation) drops its sponsorship of the Internet as AOL, CompuServe, other providers come online. EBay is launched.

1996: The Internet comes of age. Multimedia machines and digital cameras are now within reach of the average consumer.

1998: Microsoft introduced the Windows 98 browser. PayPal is launched. Google starts to gain a foothold on the search space.

2000: The dot-com crash begins. The "Millennium Bug" or "Y2K Bug" causes minor disturbances, but not the worldwide disasters some pundits foretold.

2001: Amazon.com records its first profit.

2002: Quantum computing is beginning to be explored. Hewlett-Packard merges with Compaq Computer forming the second largest IT company on earth.

2003: MySpace launches. LinkedIn launches. WordPress blogging software is launched.

2004: The Google search engine indexes 3 billion Web pages. Spam takes up an estimated 33 percent of Internet traffic. More than 650 million PCs are in use worldwide. Facebook launches. Flickr launches.

2005: Google indexes more than 8 billion Web pages, out of an estimated 11.5 billion indexable Web pages. The MIT Media Lab, in conjunction with the nonprofit association One Laptop Per Child (OLPC), launches a new research initiative to develop a $100 laptop, with the aim of revolutionizing how children worldwide are educated. YouTube launches.

2006: There are now more than 100 million Web sites on the Internet. Twitter launches. Google buys YouTube.

2008: E-commerce and online sales are estimated at $204 billion, up 17 percent from 2007.

Chapter 2

State of the Industry

While the Internet industry is young, it is growing by leaps and bounds. What was cutting-edge this year could be passé by year's end, and it is the savvy person who, when launching a career in this industry, knows how to keep it moving forward.

This chapter builds on the material discussed in Chapter 1. With an understanding of how the Internet began, the problems it was designed to handle, and how it has helped drive advances in other areas, it is often possible to anticipate and take advantage of opportunities—both today and in the future. This chapter will explore the current state of the Internet, with information on current and future trends, important technologies, key conference and industry events, key players, legal and governmental issues, and more.

Trends in Employment

The U.S. Bureau of Labor and Statistics (BLS) no longer provides information on Internet careers, per se, because the Internet has become such an integral part of so many careers that it is considered part and parcel—at least for the purposes of the BLS. Instead, the BLS combines employment statistics for computer systems analysts, database administrators, and computer scientists, which includes Web site designers. According to Education Online Search, based on the large number of people reported in this group as a whole—nearly 1 million—it is safe to assume that there are more than 100,000 Web site designers in the United States.

According to the BLS, Web site design is expected to be among the fastest growing occupations through 2012, with employment expected to grow much faster than the average. As might be expected, outsourcing is slowing down job growth and creating greater competition for available jobs; however, this should not discourage the passionate, motivated Web site designer.

The BLS does provide extensive information on computer programmers and developers. Jobs for programmers should be most plentiful in computer consulting businesses. These businesses are part of the computer systems design and related services industry, which is projected to be among the fastest-growing industries in the economy over the 2006 to 2016 period.

Prospects for advancement as a computer programmer are good—provided one keeps up-to-date with the latest technology. This is not a field for someone who does not thrive on change and who has a hard time learning to adapt. Some applications programmers may move into systems programming after they gain experience and take courses in systems software. With general business experience, programmers may become programmer-analysts or systems analysts, or may be promoted to managerial positions. Programmers with specialized knowledge and experience with a language or operating system may work in research and development, and even become computer software engineers.

Computer programmers are at a much higher risk of having their jobs outsourced than are workers involved in more complex and sophisticated functions, such as software engineering. Much of the work of computer programmers requires little localized or specialized knowledge and can be made routine once a particular programming language is mastered. The employment of computer programmers is expected to decline by 4 percent through 2016. However, because computer programmers can transmit their programs over the Internet, they can perform their job from

Fast Facts

A Growing Demographic

According to the consulting firm WomenTrend, more than 52 percent of online shoppers have been women since the year 2000. They control $7 trillion in consumer and business spending, and are now the primary purchasers of electronic equipment online.

anywhere in the world, allowing companies to employ workers in countries that have lower prevailing wages.

Nevertheless, local programmers will always be needed. Employers especially value programmers who understand how their role fits into the company's overall business and objectives. Demand will likely grow for programmers with strong object-oriented programming capabilities and technical specialization in areas such as client/server programming (writing programs that communication with other computer programs across a network), wireless applications, multimedia technology, and graphic user interface.

Despite the projected decline, numerous job openings will result from the need to replace programmers who leave the labor force or who transfer to other occupations. Prospects likely will be best for applicants with a bachelor's degree and experience with a variety of programming languages and tools. The languages that are in demand today include C++, Java, and other object-oriented languages, as well as newer, domain-specific languages that apply to computer networking, database management, and Internet application development. As always, the computer programmer who stays up-to-date on the technology is the programmer with the edge. Median annual earnings of computer programmers were $65,510 in May 2006. The middle 50 percent earned between $49,580 and $85,080 a year. The lowest 10 percent earned less than $38,460, and the highest 10 percent earned more than $106,610.

With regard to computer systems analysts, this field is expected to grow by 29 percent from 2006 to 2016. In addition, the 146,000 new jobs that are expected to arise will be substantial. Demand for systems analysts will increase as organizations adopt and integrate increasingly sophisticated technologies. One possible trend has to do with wireless capabilities and the growth of personal mobile computers—whether it's a laptop, a PDA, or a phone. These technologies have created a need for new systems that can integrate them into existing networks. Explosive growth in these areas is expected to fuel demand for analysts who are knowledgeable about systems integration and network, data, and communications security.

Job prospects in this field are expected to be good. As with computer programmers and other computer-specific positions, job openings will occur as a result of strong growth and from the need to replace workers who move into managerial positions or other occupations, or who leave the labor force. As technology becomes more sophisticated and complex, employers demand a higher level of skill and expertise from their employees. However, as with other information technology jobs, employment growth may be tempered somewhat as some analyst jobs are outsourced. Firms may look to cut costs by shifting operations to foreign countries with lower prevailing wages and highly educated workers who have strong technical skills. This is not expected to be as prevalent as with more general careers, such as computer programmers.

People with the best prospects for systems analyst positions are those with an advanced degree in computer science or computer engineering, or with an MBA with a concentration in information systems. College graduates with a bachelor's degree in computer science, computer engineering, information science, or management information systems also should enjoy favorable job prospects, particularly if they have practical experience to back up their academic learning. Median annual earnings of computer systems analysts were $69,760 in May 2006. The middle 50 percent earned between $54,320 and $87,600 a year. The lowest 10 percent earned less than $42,780, and the highest 10 percent earned more than $106,820.

Computer software engineers held about 857,000 jobs in 2006. Approximately 507,000 were computer applications software engineers, and about 350,000 were computer systems software engineers. Although they are employed in most industries, the largest concentration of computer software engineers—more than 29 percent—is in computer systems design and related services. About 17,000 computer software engineers were self-employed in 2006.

Employment of computer software engineers is projected to increase by 38 percent over the 2006 to 2016 period, which is much faster than the average for all occupations. This occupation is expected to generate about 324,000 new jobs—one of the largest employment increases of any occupation. In May 2006, median annual earnings of computer applications software engineers were $79,780. The middle 50 percent earned between $62,830 and $98,470. The lowest 10 percent earned less than $49,350, and the highest 10 percent earned more than $119,770.

Database administrators held about 119,000 jobs in May 2006. The greatest concentration of these workers is in the computer systems design and related services industry. A growing number are employed on a temporary or contract basis; many of these individuals are self-employed, working independently as contractors or consultants.

This occupation is expected to grow 37 percent from 2006 to 2016, as organizations continue to adopt and integrate increasingly sophisticated technologies. Job increases will be driven by rapid growth in computer systems design and related services, which is projected to be one of the fastest growing industries in the U.S. economy.

Those with an advanced degree in computer science or computer engineering, or with an MBA with a concentration in information systems should enjoy favorable employment prospects. Applicants with a bachelor's degree in computer science, computer engineering, information science, or management information systems (MIS) also should enjoy favorable prospects, particularly if they have supplemented their formal education with practical experience. Median annual earnings of database administrators were $64,670 in May 2006. The middle 50 percent earned between $48,560 and $84,830. The lowest 10 percent earned less than $37,350, and the highest 10 percent earned more than $103,010.

Trends in Technology

It is perhaps easiest to think of the Internet in terms of different segments or areas. For example, there are portals, e-commerce sites, nonprofit segments, and social networking. This section will examine each of these areas in turn.

Portals

A portal, as the name implies, is a gateway or entry point to somewhere else. The most common example of a portal is a search engine like Google. However, a portal can also provide access to information about a specific subject, such as stocks, news, or entertainment. In the late 1990s everyone, it seemed, was jumping on the portal bandwagon, eager to claim a share of the Internet pie. Even the Walt Disney Company tried to get in on the act with their portal, Go.com. Only a few companies, however, proved to have staying power.

There are actually two types of portals: vertical and horizontal. Google is a great example of a horizontal portal. This is a site that casts a wide net, covering a broad range of information. A vertical portal, also called a vortal, has a more narrow focus and is designed to act as an entry point for a specific niche, subject area, or interest. Horizontal portals are more often aimed at business-to-consumer (B2C) interactions. Take Amazon, for example. While it might first appear to be a vertical portal—and, indeed, in its early days, Amazon was more of a vertical portal—the site today has such a wide focus and is designed to provide such a vast array of products, from books to appliances, that it is really a horizontal portal. Vertical portals, on the other hand, are typically focused on business-to-business (B2B) interactions and are not as concerned with consumers. Move.com is a prime example of a vertical portal. This site is focused on one specific area—housing—and provides resources on buying and renting homes. The site does go into a few other areas, such as providing listings, information on moving, remodeling, and decorating. Yet, the focus is still on the one area and nothing is for sale on the site.

The volume of B2B transactions is generally much higher than the volume of B2C transactions, primarily because with B2B transactions, so many more transactions are involved in the supply chain as a desired item goes from raw material to middlemen to finished form—all before it is ready for consumption. With B2C transactions, on the other hand, there is just one exchange: the sale of the finished product to the consumer. Consider a furniture manufacturer. The manufacturer makes several B2B transactions, such as buying wood and springs for the frame and material for the upholstery. The final transaction, a finished couch or chair sold to the consumer, is a single B2C transaction.

Portals are not just focused on B2B and B2C interactions, although that is a huge segment of the portal "population." Governments, cities, agencies, and corporations all have portals. For example, a city's Web site is a portal to that city, with information on services, tourist activities, employment opportunities, and more. And there is yet one more type of portal: that between a business and its employees. B2E e-commerce uses an intranet of sorts that allows companies to provide products and/or services to their employees. Companies often use B2E networks to automate employee-related corporate processes, such as online insurance policy management, online supply requests, corporate announcements, special employee-only offers, reporting on employee benefits, and 401(k) management.

E-commerce

E-commerce, which is short for *electronic commerce*, refers to the buying and selling of goods and services. This commerce can be between businesses (B2B) or between businesses and consumers (B2C). While today, the meaning of the term might seem so obvious as to not need stating, the fact is that 30 years ago, *electronic commerce* referred to "the facilitation of commercial transactions electronically, using technology such as electronic data interchange (EDI) and electronic funds transfer (ETF)." These technologies, first introduced in the 1970s, expanded in the 1980s to include widespread use of credit cards, automatic teller machines, and telephone banking, as well as a networked airline reservation system and—the heart of e-commerce today—online shopping. (Online shopping was invented in the United Kingdom in 1979 by Michael Aldrich and, early on, was used extensively by auto manufacturers such as Ford and General Motors. Widespread commercial use of the Internet, however, was still several years off.)

Until 1991, commercial enterprise on the Internet was prohibited. The people behind the Internet—the coders, programmers, developers, engineers, and visionaries—were deeply afraid that this vast expanse of cyberspace, open to any and all possibilities, would quickly become privatized and "undone by commercialization and greed." In an article in *Electronic Engineering Times* in 1995, Jeff Johnson wrote: "Ideally, individuals and small businesses would use the information highway to communicate, but it is more likely that the information highway will be controlled by Fortune 500 companies in 10 years." Andrew Shapiro took it a step further in his July 1995 article in *The Nation:* "Speech in cyberspace will not be free if we allow big business to control every square inch of the Net." Restrictions started to crack in 1999, with the introduction of enhanced security protocols and digital subscriber line (DSL), which allowed safer, constant connection to the Internet. By the end of 2000, the fears of people like Johnson and Shapiro had been entirely swept away (although perhaps not alleviated), and many companies throughout the world were offering all sorts of goods and services through the Web.

However, this does not mean that commerce on the Internet is a free-for-all. In the United States, the Federal Trade Commission (FTC) regulates certain e-commerce activities, such as the use of commercial e-mails, online advertising, and consumer privacy. Specific examples of regulation include The CAN-SPAM Act of 2003, which establishes national standards for direct marketing through e-mail; the Federal Trade Commission Act, which regulates all forms of advertising (including online) and states that all advertising must be "truthful and nondeceptive"; and the Ryan Haight Online

Pharmacy Consumer Protection Act of 2008, which amends the Controlled Substances Act to address online pharmacies.

Although, as of this writing, the current global economic crisis has caused consumer purchases to decline, this trend is not expected to continue. Amazon is still one of the winners in this field, with fourth quarter sales in 2008 up 18 percent on a global basis. According to Plunkett Research, Ltd., top-selling products and services worldwide include travel, clothing and accessories, books, music, videos, electronics, and specialty foods, such as wines. In addition, many of the world's largest brick-and-mortar retailers operated some of the most highly trafficked Internet sites, including those run by Wal-Mart, Target, Best Buy, J.C. Penney, Sears, Home Depot, Lowes, Macy's, Kohl's, Cabela's, and Barnes and Noble.

E-commerce Strategies

In addition to portals, e-commerce strategies include direct selling, advertising, and access and licensing. At its heart, direct selling (also known as direct marketing) is exactly what it sounds like: one person selling something to another person. This is not a new concept, having been around since the dawn of commerce. While this certainly can be as simple as a person-to-person transaction on eBay or Craigslist, the Web site Directselling411.com offers a more refined definition, one that works well when applied to the Internet: "[T]he sale of a consumer product or service . . . marketed through independent sales representatives who are sometimes also referred to as consultants, distributors, or other titles. Direct sellers are not employees of the company. They are independent contractors who market and sell the products or services of a company in return for a commission on those sales." Direct selling takes place both online and offline, although the Internet has both re-energized and revolutionized it. Direct selling is a complex endeavor, and a thorough exploration of it is beyond this scope of this book. This section will take a look at the types of direct selling as it applies to the Internet, with a look at leaders and trends, but readers are encouraged to refer to Chapter 4 for an in-depth look at tips and techniques for Internet entrepreneurs and Chapter 6 for more in-depth sources of information on related topics.

Direct selling and advertising on the Internet can take several forms. For example, e-mail direct marketing targets consumers through their e-mail accounts. E-mail addresses can be harvested from Web sites, forums, or even purchased. Some companies require visitors to agree to receive promotional e-mails to use their Web sites. The three basic advertising methods used on the Internet are cost-per-click (CPC), cost-per-impressions (CPM), and cost-per-action (CPA).

E-commerce Trends

CPC advertising is the most common and is probably what most people think of when it comes to Web site advertising. With this method, an ad for one site is placed on another Web site; the owner of the first site pays a fee every time someone clicks on the ad to get to the site. These often take the form of banner ads and pop-up ads, which Internet users have increasingly little patience for; as a result, Web site owners risk paying for an ad that no one is bothering to click on. Some advertisers try to circumvent this by forcing visitors to a site to see their ad before they can get to the content they really want. The downside to this, however, is that users may get so frustrated with this that they stop coming to the site altogether. The content behind the ad must be worth the hassle. Visitors are often willing to sit through a 30-second advertisement to see a popular YouTube video, for example, but may not be willing to sit through that same ad when they want to research the prices of new cell phones.

CPM advertising runs on the same principle as CPC advertising. The difference is that advertisers are paying for a certain number (usually 1,000) of impressions (that is, appearances) of the ad on a Web site. This method, however, carries the same risks as CPC, and when determining if this is a viable advertising method, the click-through ratio must be taken into consideration. For example, compare paying $10 for 10,000 impressions versus paying 50 cents per 10 clicks, for a total of $5. If the click through rate is 1 percent, the person who paid $10 for 10,000 impressions got 100 clicks, while the person who paid 50 cents for 10 clicks got 100 clicks for $5. However, if the click-through rate on the 10,000 impressions was 3 percent, that person paid $10 for 300 clicks—a better deal than the 50 cents per 10 clicks. Danielle Babb, author of *The Online Professor's Guide to Starting an Internet Business*, has noticed an interesting trend with this CPM advertising, in which "text-based ads actually receive more attention and click-throughs than banner ads . . . we assume people would prefer to click on a graphic. But data shows that the average view time for a text-based ad is about 7.0 seconds, while the average for a graphical ad is about 1.6 seconds." CPM is also likely to work better for advertisers who use popular keywords that are more apt to be picked up by search engines and ranked high in result listings.

With CPA advertising, the advertiser does not pay for the ad unless a sale is made off it. A particular ad is put into rotation with a selection of other similar ads and is displayed as soon as it is added. Consider visiting the same Web site—say, a medical information site—and seeing an ad for an antidepressant. An hour or so later, when this same site is viewed again, there is an ad for a new arthritis medication. This is likely an example of CPA advertising. This method is suitable for an advertiser who wants to test a campaign before actually launching the ad, as it lets them see how many people actually purchase their product after viewing the ad.

The Future of Search

There is not a Web site owner out there who is not familiar with the concept of search engine optimization (SEO). Competition is fierce to be at the top of the search pile—both as a provider and in the results. Google is no doubt the reigning champion in this area, having snatched the lion's share of the search market from AltaVista, Lycos, Ask, Internet Explorer, and even Yahoo!. In May 2009, Microsoft launched a new search service called Bing. Sure, the name is catchy and the television ads are humorous, but does Bing have what it takes to knock Google off its perch? Microsoft claims that Bing can do what Google cannot—that is, help people "make faster, more informed decisions"—by combining a search engine with more organized results and unique tools to help users find the information they need. The product is being touted as a "decision engine" rather than a "search engine." The hope, according to a May 26, 2009, press release, is that users will find what they are looking for on the first try (the implication in the ads is that search engines like Google and Yahoo! do not enable users to do this). According to advertising and marketing writer Dan Leahul, however, whether Bing is better than Google in delivering results is irrelevant. Google has the power of branding on its side. The biggest hurdle for Microsoft, rather, will be to steer users away from Google altogether. And this is a monumental—perhaps impossible?—task indeed. A recent survey by *Advertising Age* revealed that users preferred search engines with the Google logo at the top of the page, regardless of the search results shown.

Stephen Wolfram, a scientist and businessman, however, wants to push the envelope of search even further by attempting to create what he calls a "computational knowledge engine." In response to users' queries, the product, known as Wolfram Alpha, will compute answers rather than Web pages. It consists of three elements: a constantly expanding collection of data sets (collections of data usually presented in tabular form), a complex calculator, and a natural-language interface for queries. For example, a search on the distance from Seattle to New York would not just provide the answer in miles, but in "kilometers and nautical miles; a map showing the flight path; and a comparison of how long it would take a jet, a sound wave, and a light beam to make the trip." A query on whether McDonald's is better than Burger King would display side-by-side charts and graphs and other analytical devices for comparison. While there are some who might say that Alpha will simply overwhelm users with more information than they know what to do with—the claim Bing is leveling against Google now—advocates of the computational knowledge engine refute that claim by saying that it is not providing information users do not want; rather, it is providing deeper, more specific, and graphically enhanced results than was previously possible. It is not just answering users' queries; it is doing so in a truly intelligent way.

Alpha is still in the early stages, and there is still a long way to go before it can give Google a run for its money, but according to Scott Kim, executive vice president for technology at Ask, "I think it opens people's eyes . . . to what you can get out of a computational engine, and how that can be integrated into a search engine . . . This is absolutely part of the future of search."

Cloud Computing

American computer scientist John McCarthy believed that "computation may someday be organized as a public utility." This involves using the Internet to meet the needs of users; it is a network of sorts that goes beyond what a traditional network is and can do. Cloud computing is designed to meet an ever-present need: more resources and an easy way to increase capacity without increasing cost. This field is still in the early stages of development, and the industry is still debating what it is, exactly, and how it can best be achieved. In one form, called "software as a service" (SaaS), it involves the distribution of a single application to thousands of users—an example is

Professional Ethics

The Right Ways of Marketing

According to SEO Book.com blogger Aaron Wall, "The difference between spam and good marketing is perception. Most techniques are not typically classified as spam until after people heavily abuse them. In other words, market timing and unique techniques are all you need to do to succeed, and that is pretty cool since new markets are always forming." While Aaron may have a point, the fact of the matter is that most people recognize spam when they see it—and make no mistake: The federal government will penalize those it deems to have committed this infraction. So how does one avoid becoming a spammer yet achieve success in advertising? Chapter 4 provides some concrete tips. In a nutshell, do not buy e-mail lists, do not send unsolicited e-mail, and always respect requests to be removed from your mailing list.

Google Apps, a single product with several services, such as e-mail, word processing, and chat, built into it. Another form, called utility computing, involves the use of virtual servers and storage areas. IT departments, for example, find these convenient—extra storage that does not take up physical space. One of the most appealing traits of cloud computing is that users do not need to have any special knowledge or skills to use the technology—it is just there, so to speak, "in the clouds."

Green IT

Practically everyone these days is aware of how important it is to recycle, to minimize the carbon footprint, to consume less, to be "green"—and computing is no different. Green IT, also called green computing, is focused on using computer resources more efficiently. The goals of green IT are to reduce the use of hazardous materials in the production of computer parts, maximize energy efficiency during a product's lifetime, and promote the creation of recyclable products and components, where possible, or even products that are biodegradable. At the same time, user satisfaction and computing ability and performance must not be sacrificed—a fine line to walk, indeed!

One of the earliest pushes in this direction was the U.S. Environmental Protection Agency's EnergyStar program. This voluntary labeling program was designed to promote and recognize energy efficiency in monitors, among other things, and resulted in the introduction and adoption of "sleep mode," whereby a computer not in use for a designated period would minimize the amount of energy it used without shutting itself completely off.

Cloud computing and green IT are linked, in a way. By making more resources virtual and minimizing the amount of energy needed to produce, package, ship, store, house, and maintain physical computers, their components, and related equipment, more can be done with less. People who are new to the computer industry and who also have a passion for the environment may find working in green IT especially appealing. Creating smaller components that are faster and more efficient, devising new materials that are not as hazardous (that perhaps are completely nontoxic), and recycling and reusing components wherever possible—even telecommuting—helps ensure that our world will be a clean, enjoyable place for years to come.

Quantum Computing

Quantum mechanics is a branch of physics that describes physical systems at the microscopic level—it deals with atomic and subatomic systems. In fact, it was designed to provide a better explanation of the atom. The field of quantum computing is still very much in its infancy, but by harnessing these principles into a computer, the hope is that quantum computers will be able to perform calculations millions of times faster than traditional computers. Unlike silicon-based computers, quantum computers would use the power of atoms and molecules to perform calculations and carry out tasks. Traditional computers operate in two states—the binary system, in which information is represented as either a 1 or a 0. Quantum computers, on the other hand are not limited to two states; they encode information as quantum bits (qubits), which represent atoms, ions, photons, or electrons. Because a quantum computer can contain multiple states simultaneously, it has the potential to be millions of times more powerful than today's most powerful supercomputers.

The Organizations That Steer the Internet

Technology author Alex Simonelis is absolutely correct when he says that "certain protocols, and the parameters required for their usage, are essential in order to operate on the Internet." Several organizations have become responsible for these standards and practices.

➜ **Internet Architecture Board:** Established in 1992, this body is designed to "oversee the architecture of the Internet, including its protocols and other standards."

➜ **Internet Assigned Numbers Authority:** This group's origins go back to the 1970s, and it is part of the Internet Corporation for Assigned Names and Numbers. IANA "oversees IP address allocation, manages the domain name system (DNS), and coordinates protocol parameter assignments." All Internet domain names and IP addresses are issued from it, whether directly or indirectly.

➜ **Internet Corporation for Assigned Names and Numbers:** ICANN was chartered in 1998 and receives the authorization to perform its duties from the U.S. Department of Commerce. Its directives are to "coordinate the assignment of Internal technical parameters as needed to maintain universal connectivity on the Internet; perform and oversee functions related to the coordination of IP address space; perform and oversee functions related to the coordination of the Internet DNS, including the development of policies for determining [when] new top-level domains are added to the root system; and oversee the operation of the authoritative DNS root server system."

➜ **Internet Engineering Steering Group:** The IESG was formed in 1989 as part of the Internet Engineering Task Force. It "vets and approves IETF standards and generally manages the standards process according to the policies and procedures ratified by Internet Society trustees."

➜ **Internet Engineering Task Force:** Founded in 1986, the IETF is a grassroots technical group comprising network administrators, designers, researchers, vendors, users, and others. It is not a formal body, per se, but rather operates under the auspices of the Internet Society. Practically anyone who wants to join can, as membership is informal and participation is on a voluntary basis. The

IETF is concerned with the engineering and architecture of the Internet. It is "the principal body that develops, tests, and implements new Internet technological standards, including protocols."

→ **Internet Research Task Force:** Formed in 1989, the focus of the IRTF is—as the name implies—research. It "investigates Internet topics that are too uncertain or too advanced to be standardized at the moment." When IRTF produces a specification that is suitable for standardization, it is processed by the Internet Engineering Task Force.

→ **Internet Society:** The ISOC was founded in 1991 and welcomes both individuals and organizations as its members. It was formed in response to the Internet's astounding growth during that time and to fill a need for a formal organization to provide a "legal" home for various standards bodies. Its mission is "to assure the open development, evolution, and use of the Internet for the benefit of all people throughout the world."

→ **RFC Editor:** Requests for comments (RFCs) are documents published by the Internet Engineering Task Force describing methods, behaviors, research, or innovations applicable to the working of the Internet and Internet-connected systems. The RFC Editor is the organization that edits, manages, publishes, and maintains the official archive of RFC documents, which are the Internet's "documents of record."

→ **World Wide Web Consortium:** The W3C was founded in 1994 by Tim Berners-Lee. Its mission is "to lead the World Wide Web to its full potential by developing common protocols that promote its evolution and ensure its interoperability." The W3C develops, tests, and implements new Web technological standards.

The Companies Behind (and in Front) of the Trends

Many, many companies help forge new trends on the Internet, or take advantage of the trends forged by others. Some go on to become widely influential; others are influential in a much smaller sphere. This section highlights a few of the most well known. A complete treatment of all the companies involved would fill a book in itself.

Chapter 6 provides more information on some companies. The Internet can certainly fill in any other gaps.

Adobe Systems

According to information on the Adobe Systems Web site, as of February 2009, Adobe had 7,173 employees, about 40 percent of whom worked in San Jose, California (the company's headquarters). Adobe also had major development operations in Seattle, Washington; San Francisco, California; Ottawa, Ontario; Minneapolis, Minnesota; Newton, Massachusetts; San Luis Obispo, California; Hamburg, Germany; Noida, India; Bangalore, India; Bucharest, Romania; and Beijing, China. In 2003, *Fortune* magazine rated Adobe as the fifth-best U.S. company to work for; however, by 2009, it had slipped to number 11.

Amazon.com, Inc.

The company that single-handedly changed the way the world buys books, Amazon emerged on the Web in 1995. By 1997, it was the first retailer to secure 1 million customers. Today, it claims to offer "Earth's biggest selection" of not only books, but also CDs, DVDs, electronics, toys, tools, home furnishings and housewares, apparel, and kitchen gadgets. Through third-party agreements, Amazon sells products from retailers such as Toys R Us and Target. The company is headquartered in Seattle, Washington, and as of 2009 had 20,700 employees. Its reported revenue in 2008 was over $19 billion.

Apple, Inc.

Apple is best known for its Macintosh computer, iPod, and iPhone, but it also produces the Mac OS X operating system, the iTunes media browser, the iLife suite of multimedia and creativity software, the iWork suite of productivity software, and Final Cut Studio, a suite of professional audio and film-industry software products. The competition between Apple and Microsoft has certainly extended to its consumers, with devoted fans singing the praises of Apple—and the pitfalls of Windows—to anyone who will listen. Whether you are a Mac or a PC, there is no denying the company is a presence in the industry, and likely to remain so. Headquartered in Cupertino, California, Apple has about 35,000 employees worldwide, according to an October 21, 2008 press release, and had worldwide annual sales of $32.48 billion in its fiscal year ending September 29, 2008. In 2008, *Fortune* magazine named Apple the most admired company in the United States after polling more than 3,700 people from dozens of industries on the companies they admire most.

Dell, Inc.

Headquartered in Round Rock, Texas, Dell currently employs more than 82,700 worldwide and earned $61.133 billion in revenue in 2008. As of 2008, Dell was second in computer sales behind Hewlett Packard (HP). Dell currently sells personal computers, servers, data storage devices, network switches, software, and computer peripherals, as well as HDTVs (high-definition TVs) that are manufactured by other brands.

Dell now has the second-largest market share of any computer manufacturer, a position it carved out for itself starting in the year 2000. As competition increased among computer manufacturers, the company was founded on the notion that by selling PCs directly to the consumer, the consumer's needs could be better understood, thereby providing them with the most effective computing solution. It is a belief that has served the company well. Between the second quarter of fiscal year 2001 and second quarter of fiscal year 2002, Dell's market share grew from 12.8 percent to 14.8 percent. At the same time, the combined market share of Hewlett-Packard and Compaq slipped from 17.9 percent to 15.1 percent. According to a 2006 press release, Dell is one of 38 high-performance companies in the S&P 500 that has consistently outperformed the market over the previous 15 years.

eBay, Inc.

eBay was born in 1995 when a computer programmer named Pierre Omidyar wrote the code for an auction Web site that he ran from his home computer. The very first item sold on eBay was a broken laser pointer for $14.83. When the astonished Omidyar contacted the winning bidder to ask if he understood that the laser pointer was broken, the buyer explained that he collected broken laser pointers. (And you thought people who collected spoons or salt and pepper shakers were weird!) With a presence in 39 markets, including the United States, and approximately 84 million active users worldwide, eBay has certainly changed the face of Internet commerce. In 2007, the total value of items sold on the site's trading platforms was nearly $60 billion. That breaks to an interesting piece of trivia: eBay users worldwide trade more than $1,900 worth of goods on the site every second! The company is headquartered in San Jose, California, and had 15,500 employees in 2008. Reported revenue for that year was over $8.5 billion.

Google, Inc.

Headquartered in Mountain View, California (the name of Google's headquarters is the Googolplex), as of December 31, 2008, the company had 20,222 full-time employees, according to a press release issued in January 2009, and *Fortune* magazine has ranked it as the number one place to work, most recently in 2007. One of the most recognizable brand names today, Google earns its money from advertising related to its Internet search, e-mail, online mapping, office productivity, social networking, and video sharing services, as well as selling advertising-free versions of the same technologies. When Google emerged as an Internet search engine, the concept behind it was revolutionary—namely, that the pages with the most links to them from other highly relevant Web pages must be the most relevant pages associated with the search. According to recent annual reports, 99 percent of Google's revenue is derived from its advertising programs. For the 2006 fiscal year, the company reported $10.492 billion in total advertising revenues and $112 million in licensing and other revenues. While the company has been criticized for its below-average pay, the competitive compensation packages offered are viewed by some to offset this.

IBM

With a history dating back to the nineteenth century, International Business Machines (IBM) has earned its reputation as the world's largest computer company and the second largest software company. According to the company's Web site, IBM has more than 388,000 employees in more than 170 countries, eight research laboratories worldwide, and holds more patents than any other U.S.-based technology company. IBM employees have earned three Nobel Prizes, four Turing Awards, five National Medals of Technology, and five National Medals of Science.

Microsoft Corporation

Microsoft, headquartered in Redmond, Washington, has been the target of criticism for its monopoly-like business practices, but no one can doubt the company's clout. According to the company's annual report for 2005, Microsoft's reach extends to the MSNBC cable television network and the MSN Internet portal, and the company markets both computer hardware products, such as the Microsoft

On the Cutting
Edge

Telecommuting

So will the majority of jobs all be online some day? The trend is certainly moving in that direction. While it is not likely that all workers will be working from home all the time, according to journalist Eve Tahmincioglu about six million workers telecommuted more than eight hours week in 2000, but by 2009 that number hit an estimated 14 million. Caroline Jones, an analyst for Gartner who expects the number to continue to grow, says the rate of increase has been steady for a number of years. Technology has been one of the biggest motivators in this area, particularly advances in wireless and mobile technology, video conferencing, and Web cams. Then there are the savings costs to employers. At Sun Microsystems, for example, more than 56 percent of employees work without an assigned office, which means they either work from home or use flexible office space. Employees work in three categories under what Sun calls the Open Work program: (1) Sun assigned: an employee has an assigned office on one of Sun's campuses; (2) flexible: an employee works out of flexible offices, drop-in centers, or from home whenever they choose; and (3) home assigned: the employee works from home. The program has led to $387 million in IT and real estate savings.

Telecommuting is not for everyone, of course. Some people just do not have the discipline to work outside of a traditional office setting, and some jobs simply do not lend themselves well to the concept. But even in these cases, if technology can make telecommuting possible, the motivated employee could make a case for it to his or her boss.

mouse, and home entertainment products, such as the Xbox, Xbox 360, Zune, and MSN TV. According to the Microsoft Web site, as of December 31, 2008, the company employed 95,828 people worldwide, 57,588 of whom were in the United States. In 2005, Microsoft received a 100 percent rating in the Corporate Equality Index from the Human Rights Campaign, a ranking of companies by how progressive the organization deems their policies concerning lesbian, gay, bisexual, and transsexual employees.

Oracle Corporation

Oracle Corporation is perhaps best known for its eponymous database management system, but the company also builds tools for database development, middle-tier software, enterprise resource planning software (ERP), customer relationship management software (CRM), and supply chain management (SCM) software. Headquartered in the Bay Area near San Francisco, the company employs an estimated 85,000 people worldwide according to the Oracle Web site. Oracle has earned its place in the computing industry pantheon through organic growth combined with high-profile, well-timed acquisitions, like BEA and Hyperion. Oracle competes for new database licenses on UNIX, Linux, and Windows operating systems primarily against IBM's DB2 and Microsoft SQL Server; however, IBM's DB2 still dominates the mainframe database market. Initially, Oracle was on friendly terms with German company SAP AG, the world's second largest business software company and the third-largest independent software provider (in terms of revenue), but this cooperation has devolved over the years to an outright rivalry. On March 22, 2007, Oracle sued SAP AG, accusing them of fraud and unfair competition (the case is set to go to trial in November 2010).

Yahoo!, Inc.

The company's two founders, David Filo and Jerry Yang, Ph.D. candidates in electrical engineering at Stanford University, started Yahoo! in 1994 as a way to keep track of their personal interests on the Internet. When these lists eventually become unwieldy and hard to manage, the two young men broke them out into categories, and subcategories, and soon the Web site was officially born. The origins of the name are twofold. Some claim that Yahoo is an acronym for "Yet Another Hierarchical Officious Oracle," but Filo and

Yang claim they selected the word because of its general definition: "rude, unsophisticated, uncouth." Regardless of how the name came about, the company behind it was founded in 1995. It is headquartered in Santa Clara, California, and boasts 13,500 employees and in 2008 reported $7 billion in revenue. Recent offerings in addition to search include online business and enterprise services such as an enterprise portal solution, audio and video streaming, store hosting and management, and Web site tools and services.

A Few More Companies to Watch

In March 2009, Gartner Research compiled a list of several vendors to keep an eye on in the coming months for "the way they could aid in cost optimization, operational performance and organizational skill development initiatives." These names encompass a wide variety of segments of the computing industry. For example:

- Skytap, a venture-backed company based in Seattle, Washington, provides virtual labs for application development and QA teams. Developers can access these virtual labs and use Skytap's library of prebuilt virtual machines, operating systems, and application images; alternatively, they can upload existing virtual machines, builds, or test scripts into the Skytap environment.
- LogLogic is a company that enables log data from firewalls, routers, servers, applications, operating systems, and other devices to be automatically collected, stored, reported, and alerted on in near real-time because "bandwidth reduction and greater safeguards against internal and external threats via log management will result in cost."
- RollStream, Inc. provides a suite of on-demand collaboration tools that allows IT managers to reduce the time and effort required to collaborate and communicate with suppliers or customers on large projects.
- NextPlane lets business users communicate through instant messaging and collaborate, regardless of the underlying unified communications platform or service.
- G2G3, one of the leading providers of simulation programs, recently partnered with IBM to produce the

Virtual Service Management Simulator, an immersive 3D learning system where participants learn how service management and IT infrastructure library (ITIL) processes can be applied to improve business performance.

Where to Spot the Trends

When it comes to conferences, the knowledge you gain there can often give you an edge in advancing your career—not to mention the networking opportunities. Looking for conferences you cannot afford to miss? Look at key ones that drive technology agendas—VoiceCon, for example. This conference is "designed to help you decide why, when and how to invest in IP telephony, and how to leverage your enterprise communications platform for maximum advantage." Go to conferences aimed at chief technology officers (CTOs), as well as industry-related conferences, such as NetWorld. NetWorld is hosted by Interop, which "is the leading business technology event series. Through in-depth educational programs, workshops, real-world demonstrations . . . Interop provides the forum for the most powerful innovations and solutions the industry has to offer."

The Electronic Entertainment Expo (http://www.e3expo.com) is one of the biggest, most important conventions a person in this field can attend. It is usually held in May in Los Angeles. This annual trade show is produced by IDSA, the publishers' trade association. While the conference is aimed at publishers and distributors, giving them an opportunity to showcase their latest games to retailers, developers often attend as well.

The National Computer Conference is the largest annual computer show in the data processing industry and is sponsored by the American Federation of Information Processing Societies (AFIPS).

CeBIT is the largest technology exposition. Held annually in Hannover, Germany, this trade show "showcases digital IT and telecommunications solutions for home and work environments. The key target groups are users from industry, the wholesale/retail sector, skilled trades, banks, the services sector, government agencies, science and all users passionate about technology." CeBIT is considered the "world's largest and most renowned trade fair for the world of IT and telecommunications."

The Computex trade show in Taipei, Taiwan, is the world's second-largest computer fair behind CeBIT, with such noteworthy participants as Intel, AMD, ATI, and NVIDIA. Taiwan's IT industry has

INTERVIEW

Social Networking May Be the New Thing, but Traditional Business Models Still Apply

Shaun Wolfe
President and CEO TangoWire Corporation, Seattle, Washington

What was your introduction to the Internet, and what caused you to establish a career in this field?
Prior to buying TangoWire (a network of more than 3,500 Web sites encompassing more than 70 online dating communities) in July 2008, I had spent 25 years in enterprise software. After a successful run with this, I was looking for a new challenge. I wanted to stay within technology, but move into Internet-based products—preferably B2C. The move was all about being challenged and doing something completely different within the technology.

Have you seen the "hot areas" in this industry change over time or have they remained relatively the same? What are these "hot areas" in your opinion?
Social networking and mobile integration are the hot areas in my mind. But I mean social networking beyond Facebook. Social networking will permeate all of our activities and technology. Whether I am buying a ticket to a movie or play, or visiting my corner grocery store, I will expect to have the opportunity to tie into a related community. For example, I might want to see a summary of reviews from everyday folks who saw the play or just my friends, or maybe people I do not know but I've come to trust their opinions. Or maybe I provide a quick review myself just after the play is over. We will see the same basic idea with the grocery store—"great meat department, but the produce sucks and no organic selection to speak of."

Anyway, 15 years from now, I do not believe we will even talk about "social networking" or "social media." It will just permeate the way we do business and conduct our personal lives. Current social networks will become platforms. You see the early days of this with Facebook, as people are building gaming and commerce applications right on it—or the iPhone. I know one nonprofit that scrapped plans to build a Web site for their community and are building a Facebook application instead.

How did you go from an enterprise software architect (ESA) to CEO of an online dating company? Are the two things more similar than a person might think?

There probably are more similarities than people think. Good business is good business. The way you treat employees and work with suppliers is no different. The philosophies around customer service can be very much the same. But what drew me to this were the things that *are* different. Running a company where the average sale is $50 and the average time-to-decision is often less than a minute carries different challenges than when a sale can be worth millions of dollars and decisions can take more than a year. There are no PowerPoint presentations in the Internet B2C business arena. There are no gatekeepers (e.g., IT departments) between you and the decision-maker. Internet B2C sales are driven by marketing, while enterprise software sales are a slave to sales cycles. Neither of these are better or worse than the other, just different. As a result, the business strategies are wildly different and decisions about which business risks to take are different.

What opportunities does the Internet offer career-wise that were not available before, or how has it changed opportunities?

The days of small, nimble enterprise software companies are slowly coming to a permanent end. Fortune 500 companies do not want mission-critical information and processes to rest on the back of a 10-person startup backed by a venture capitalist. Also, 10-person startup companies backed by a venture capitalist cannot afford six- and 12-month sales cycles.

The career-opportunities in the Internet B2C world are tremendous for entrepreneurs, marketers, and creative developers. For entrepreneurs, great ideas can be brought to market by small nimble companies to huge success in the Internet market—particularly B2C. For example, a consumer may want their tax application, banking application, data backup, and virus protection to come from a well-established, trusted company, but they do not have that same requirement for most online services and applications. For marketers, the Internet is untamed and fast-paced. Data can be collected in real time, price tests completed in hours or days, and adjustments be made overnight.

What is the most important thing someone needs to know who is considering entering the Internet industry, regardless of the specific area they end up in?

The Internet industry is ever-changing. What you know today may not apply tomorrow. You have to keep revisiting your assumptions,

(continues on next page)

INTERVIEW

Social Networking May Be the New Thing, but Traditional Business Models Still Apply (continued)

testing your theories, reading and learning, and trying everything new. But—and this is the trick—while keeping up with all the "great new things," remember that most are fads and all are overhyped at some point. Keeping the "gold rush" mentality at bay and focusing on real value is the trick.

What do you consider the biggest myth about the Internet, if any?
The biggest myth about the Internet is that standard business rules do not apply. Business models still have to make sense. Everything cannot be free and still have value.

become a driving force in the global market. Since many businesses that operate on a global scale have research and deployment centers or production facilities in Taiwan, Computex is one of the key places to discover the latest technologies, developments, and trends.

VoiceCon is a yearly conference with the aim of helping IT professionals build an IP telephony platform that is right for their business and how to leverage it for maximum business advantage. Presentations are conducted by the leading experts, vendors, and enterprise IT executives who will share their knowledge, experience, and expertise.

The Combined Exhibition of Advanced Technologies (CEATEC) is an annual trade show held in October in Makuhari Messe, Japan. Regarded as the Japanese equivalent of the Consumer Electronics Show, CEATEC has become Japan's largest IT and electronics exhibition and conference. In 2007, it drew 205,859 people, of which 165,303 were attendees, 38,705 were exhibitors, and 1,851 were press, according to official figures. Such numbers confirmed CEATAC's place as one of the world's largest consumer electronics fairs.

SIGGRAPH, held annually and hosted by the Special Interest Group of the Association for Computing Machinery, is aimed primarily at graphics designers and animators, and the other artists of the Internet world. There are also several different seminars, trade shows, and networking opportunities to take advantage of. Graphics programmers are strongly encouraged to attend this conference. Specific information can be obtained at Siggraph.org.

The Consumer Electronics Show (http://www.cesweb.org) is the largest of its kind. The focus is on games as well as consumer electronics in general. Of late, it has been surpassed by E3, which is aimed exclusively at gaming. However, it may still be of use to programmers, designers, and the like.

Digital Hollywood is one of the largest trade shows for those in the entertainment and technology industry, with an emphasis on digital media. Past speakers have included Nolan Bushnell (founder of Atari), Robert Kotick (CEO and president of Activision), Bing Gordon (former CCO of Electronic Arts), and Rob Glaser (founder of Real Networks). Information on locations, dates, events, and more can be found at Digitalhollywood.com.

For people specifically interested Microsoft products, there is TechEd. This conference is aimed at "any and all technology professionals interested in exploring a broad set of current and upcoming Microsoft technologies, tools, platforms, and services." Microsoft also offers conferences on specific products. Organization-wise, there are often user groups where you meet face to face. Following virtual communities via blogs can be good, as long as the author is credible.

Every large company like Microsoft typically has an annual conference, plus some sort of local user community. At the Google I/O Developer Conference, for example, participants will "have a chance to interact directly with the engineering teams who work on our [application programming interfaces] APIs and developer products. [D]ozens of in-depth technical sessions focus on how to write better applications using Google and open technologies." There are sessions and demos for developers who are working on business applications, as well as items of interest for the developer community, such as applications that use the latest Web and mobile technologies. And then there's the Macworld Conference & Expo. Macworld is considered the largest annual Mac gathering in the world, and the most important annual trade exposition for Apple and all Mac hardware and software vendors.

Finally, various computer-related industries often put on conferences. The IEEE, for example, offers workshops, seminars, and conferences throughout the year. Colleges, universities, and technical schools also will have information on upcoming conferences, and counselors or advisors at these schools may even be able to suggest which ones will benefit you the most.

The Future

So where will the Internet go from here, and what new changes will it bring to our lives? Some things can be gleaned from recent and emerging trends; however, just as no one could have predicted the Internet 50 years ago, 50 from years now, we may be marveling over technological innovations just as amazing and just as life-altering as the Internet itself. Nearly everyone will be on the Web, using it in their daily lives in both significant and not-so-significant ways. Technology author Kevin Kelly asks, "If everyone is busy making, altering, mixing, and mashing . . . who will be a consumer?" The answer: No one. And maybe that is the future of the Internet, a network of social creation that the futurist Alvin Toffler calls prosumption. We are both the producer and the consumer. "The producers are the audience, the act of making is the act of watching, and every link is both a point of departure and a destination." And the biggest projected leap for the Internet? It will become the operating system on which the world runs. Sun Microsystems' John Gage described this as "a megacomputer that encompasses the Internet, all its services, peripheral chips and affiliated devices, from scanners to satellites, and the billions of human minds entangled in this global network." This may be an exhilarating thought, a scary thought, or both, depending on one's perspective. Only time will tell how it manifests for sure. In the meantime, Chapter 3 offers a look at the varied aspects of Internet-related careers as they exist today.

Chapter 3

On the Job

The Internet has not only changed the way the world works, it has created employment sectors that no one could have even imagined 20 or 30 years ago. Some of the jobs discussed in this chapter are not directly related to the Internet; however, they involve the technology upon which the Internet is based—consider programming, design, manufacturing, and technical support. Other jobs, like teaching, writing, editing, composing, drawing, and selling, while certainly not new, can now occur in new arenas. Consider the fact that telecommuting, for example, was virtually unheard of before the advent of the Internet. Where possible, specific career paths and connections between certain areas are provided, but do not consider these routes the only possibility. Salary ranges are also included in cases where this information was available. Sometimes, a person starts on in one career track but then ends up an unrelated one, whether through chance or changing interests. In-depth information can be found in some of the resources listed in Chapter 6 as well as in the U.S. Bureau of Labor Statistics *Occupational Outlook Handbook* (2008–2009).

Creative Jobs

The positions in this section allow people to explore and express their creativity in a variety of ways, whether that be with words, pictures, or sound. Some of the positions discussed here have simply moved from the "real world" to the Internet, making use of its related technology. Some are focused on specific things, like software programs or Web sites.

Advertising Designer

Advertising is a huge, nearly inescapable, fact of life on the Internet. From pop-up ads to banner ads to sponsored links to programs like Google's AdWords, people who understand this new frontier of advertising and can grab the attention of someone surfing the Web can do well for themselves. Internet advertising designers, like their traditional print counterparts, are responsible for creating effective advertising for Web sites, often combining text, animation, and sound. Because Internet advertising designers need to know how effective their ads are, they often work closely with other members of the marketing department, Web site designers, and programmers. People in this field may start out in graphic design and eventually move into management, or may find more success working in a freelance capacity. Related fields include Web site design, applications programming, and technical writing.

Animator

This category includes 3-D modelers and 3-D artists. Modelers sculpt anything and everything that will appear in a video game with regard to people, buildings, creatures, and other objects. They typically start with a concept sketch (think of it as a rough draft of the piece of art) and then build a 3-D wireframe model of the particular object. Then a texture is applied to the model. If the object is not going to be animated, the modeler's job typically ends there. If the object is going to be animated, however, it goes to the 3-D animator.

As one might expect, this position is seen primarily in the video game industry; however, an animator might also be employed to create streaming content for a Web site, for example, or Flash animation.

Composer

The composer is responsible for overseeing and creating any original music employed in a software product—usually a video game, but where there is animation or video on a site, there is often music. In addition, some sites play a music file as a way of enhancing the user's experience on the site. This person has a strong background

Fast Facts

Growth in the Supersector

According to the U.S. Bureau of Labor Statistics, employment in the information supersector is expected to increase by 6.9 percent, adding 212,000 jobs by 2016. This area contains some of the fastest-growing industries, such as software publishing, Internet publishing and broadcasting, and wireless telecommunication carriers. Employment in these industries is expected to grow by 32 percent, 44.1 percent, and 40.9 percent, respectively. The information supersector also includes motion picture production; broadcasting; and newspaper, periodical, book, and directory publishing. Increased demand for telecommunications services, cable service, high-speed Internet connections, and software will fuel job growth among these industries.

in actually playing at least one instrument, but is also well versed in the equipment and software used to digitally create music. Since much music is created using a synthesizer, people who are proficient playing and composing music on the piano may have an advantage in this profession.

Computer-Aided Design Technician/Manager

Computer-aided design (CAD) is a software program used by engineers and designers to create detailed design drawings, with information on specifications, cost, dimensions, part numbers, and more. These software programs enable CAD technicians to easily make changes to plans, as well as shift or rotate them on the virtual page, which provides better visualization of a product's structure and function, for example. These technicians often work in the automotive, architecture, electronic, mechanical engineering, and other industries. While this person may not be working for an Internet-based company, per se, this is a position that could lend itself well to telecommuting. People in this field typically start at an assistant-level or drafter position and are promoted to a senior-level position, eventually becoming a manager of a CAD team or another management position. Related fields include technical writing, technical editing, hardware design, and systems design.

Computer Graphic Artist

This person designs computer-generated art or images for a multitude of purposes: Web sites, computer games, multimedia presentations, and more. When entering this field, a person may start as a technician, doing routine work scanning, manipulating, and otherwise working with graphics images, including digital photos. As skills are acquired and techniques refined, a person will move from graphics artist/designer to perhaps the director of an art department in a company. Related fields include computer game design and programming.

Desktop Publisher

A desktop publisher is responsible for designing, creating, and laying out all sorts of documents, including fact sheets, brochures, pamphlets, magazines, books, and everything in between. While they often work with writers and editors, some desktop publishers take these tasks on themselves. Many desktop publishers work in a freelance capacity. Others work in print shops or production departments of publishers, advertising agencies, or public relations firms. When working for a particular company, a person may start out as an assistant and move up as they gain experience, eventually managing a publications department, for example. Related fields include word processing, technical writing and editing, Web site design, and multimedia development.

Electronic Sound Producer

This is the person responsible for the auditory components of a computer game or multimedia presentation. Such people may use live recording, sound archives, synthesized music, and more when creating sound effects. Advancement in this field generally is linear, from entry-level to senior-level positions. At a high level, some producers manage engineers and technicians. Others may go on to become director of an art department or even become a consultant. Related fields include computer game design, animation, graphics, and multimedia development.

Flash Designer

Flash is a multimedia platform commonly used to create animation, advertisements, and various Web page components; to integrate video into Web pages; and, more recently, to develop rich Internet applications. Flash designers use this technology and combine it with a powerful scripting language, known as ActionScripting, and compressed vector output to create fast-leading, streaming content for the Internet. This animation can include images, shapes, text, and SWF (Shockwave Flash) clips for Web sites. This is a mid-level position, between an entry-level graphics designer or commercial graphic artist and the higher-level art director or producer. The salary range is between $40,000 and $80,000, and people in this field generally have at least a two-year degree (a four-year degree is better) in graphic design and fine arts, as well as experience in multimedia design, applications programming, and user interface design.

Internet Store Manager/Entrepreneur

Perhaps the best example of this is Amazon.com or eBay; however, individuals can set up and run a business on the Internet, too—sometimes with a great deal of success! Someone who is considering this endeavor certainly has a lot of responsibility, just like any other business owner. They are responsible for handling all aspects of the business: accounts receivable, accounts payable, shipping, invoicing, ordering product (if necessary), and more. Furthermore, this person is responsible for designing the Web site, as well as marketing and advertising. The fortunate entrepreneur who is just starting out may have the funds to hire people to do these tasks, but this is not typically the case. People who are successful in this field may expand the services or goods offered, or may collaborate with other businesses or Internet service providers. Related fields include interactive advertising designer, sales, and computer programming (knowledge of HTML is helpful).

Multimedia Developer/Producer

These are the people responsible for designing and programming—and in some cases overseeing—interactive multimedia projects. As the name implies, multimedia refers to something that combines audio, images, and text. Consider an interactive encyclopedia, for example. There is the text of the articles, pictures of the subjects, and perhaps a short video showing how something works. Just as with most career paths, people in this field typically start in an entry-level position, perhaps as an assistant, and move up through the ranks, from lead developer to producer, and then into a director or other management position. Some people also experience success working in a freelance capacity, but must have established a proven track record first. Related fields include Web site design, software applications, multimedia, and project management.

Multimedia or Game Writer/Editor

These are the people who write and edit the text that accompanies multimedia presentations or games. This can include a wide range of items, including articles, instructions, scripts, and descriptions, among other things. They often work with graphic artists, anima-tors, programmers, and sound or special effects producers. People do not often enter this field as a writer. They typically start as an editorial assistant or some other position and then take advantage of writing opportunities as they arise until they are promoted to an actual position as writer or editor. From there, they may become a project editor or manager. Writers who establish especially note-worthy reputations may find success as a freelancer. Related fields include technical writing and editing.

Technical Editor

Technical editors are responsible for ensuring the accuracy of techni-cal writing. This may include basic copyediting skills, like checking grammar, spelling, and punctuation, but also can include ensuring that the material the writer has produced is well organized, easy to understand, accurate, and thorough. Most of the time, techni-cal editors work closely with technical writers, but they can also work with developers, programmers, and project managers. They also work with the graphics or production departments to make sure that screen images and diagrams are laid out properly. Techni-cal editors can work in a freelance capacity, which is often the case with software publishers or trade publishers, or they may work for a publications department in a specific company. Someone seeking to become a technical editor may start with a company as an editorial assistant first, then advance to become a senior-level editor, and then from there into management. Managing editors who work for a computer book publisher often worked first as a technical editor. Related fields include technical writing, multimedia development, Web site design, and project management.

Technical Writer

Technical writers create a wide range of materials: books, manuals, documents, online help systems, tutorials, reference books, and more. They are also responsible for writing text that appears within a user interface—tooltips, for example, or the text that appears in pop-up messages or dialog boxes. They can work for trade publishers, software companies, information technology departments, or independently. If they work for a software company, they often have to work with the development team and programmers, staying in the loop about how a program is supposed to work, what its features are, how they can best meet users' needs, and so on. Technical writers who work on a freelance basis can take their career in nearly any direction they choose, provided they are motivated and self-disciplined enough. Technical writers working for a company may advance to a position where they are a lead writer, supervising other writers, or even to manager of a publications department. Related fields include technical editing, Web site design, and desktop publisher.

Virtual Reality Designer/Programmer

Virtual reality—a simulated version of the world we experience around us, including sights, sounds, and sensations—is an intriguing aspect of computer science. Developers and programmers who choose to focus on this area may help develop games, virtual tours of museums or other historical sites (past and present), or simulations for people like astronauts and airline pilots. They typically work with researchers, other programmers and developers, and engineers. Unlike many of the other positions discussed in this chapter, there is not a real career ladder, per se, in virtual reality. Naturally, it is possible to become promoted into a senior or lead position; however, from there, people often move into the academic world, becoming a professor or working in research. Related fields include computer game design and programming.

Technical Jobs

The positions in this section may be what a lot of people initially think of when they think of Internet-related jobs. To be sure, they are jobs that did not exist before computers (and then the Internet) entered our lives. They can be broad in scope, or have a narrow focus, or both.

Artificial Intelligence Programmer

Artificial intelligence—the field of computer programming that attempts to give machines the ability to reason, think, and learn like humans, using natural language—is a highly interesting, cutting-edge area of computer programming. People in this field design and implement systems that perform complex tasks, such as decision making and recognizing patterns. Practical applications include systems that are used in scheduling freight shipments, diagnosing disease, or checking credit; pattern recognition systems that can match faces seen in cameras to a database of criminal or terrorist suspects; and neural network programs that can learn to perform tasks by reevaluating performance. (A neural network is a web of interconnecting programming constructs that mimic the properties of biological neurons.)

This multidisciplinary field draws on such diverse disciplines as computer science, philosophy, linguistics, and psychology. Some people work purely in a research capacity, creating systems that demonstrate the validity of their theories; others work on a more practical level, using these systems to solve real-world problems. People who enter this field typically start at the intern or trainee level, become a programmer, then a researcher, and then someone who directs artificial intelligence projects. Related fields include data mining, engineering, and systems design.

Bioinformatics Specialist

People in this field typically organize and manipulate information relating to such things as genetic sequences, molecular structures, and other areas of biology. They create and maintain databases of this information and then make them available to biological and medical researchers. One of the more interesting areas has to do with analyzing genetic sequences and predicting their relationship to the structure and function of living things. This is one area where computers are particularly superior to humans—they can calculate in minutes what would take a human years.

Entry-level workers typically start as an associate and move up the ranks to a senior level, finally becoming a director, perhaps of a bioinformatics department or lab. People in this field often find jobs in university laboratories, organizations like the World Health Organization (WHO) or the Centers for Disease Control and Prevention (CDC), or for pharmaceutical companies. Related fields include database analysis, data mining, statistics, and programming.

Computer Hardware Designer/Engineer

These designers and engineers are responsible for producing central processing units (CPUs), memory chips, circuitry, and other computer components. They may work with software programmers and testers in order to make their products more efficient. A career path in this area typically starts at an entry-level position, and then advances to a senior-level status, eventually becoming a lead engineer. Or, this person may choose to become a department manager or project manager. Related fields include embedded systems design and robotics engineering.

Computer Hardware Manufacturing Technician

These technicians often work under designers and engineers, testing the designs or hardware components, making sure they work as intended and that there are no unforeseen problems. Often, this involves actually building the components they are testing. People in this field generally start in an assistant-level position, performing routine tests. As experience and proficiency is gained, someone in this field can expect to advance to a senior or supervisory position. Alternatively, a person may make the switch to engineering. Related fields include service technician, technical support, hardware manufacturing and design, engineering, and systems integration.

Computer Programmers

As might be expected, computer programmers conceive, design, write, test, and maintain programs. Many technical innovations in programming, such as advanced computing technologies and sophisticated new languages and programming tools, have changed the role of a programmer and elevated much of the programming work done today.

Job titles and descriptions can vary, depending on the organization. After software engineers and analysts design software and describe how it will work, the programmer converts that design into a logical series of instructions that the computer can follow. The programmer does this by "translating" the instructions into one of the many programming languages available—the language used depends on the ultimate goal of the program. If you decide to launch a career as a computer programmer, it is best to learn more than one language. This is relatively easy to do since many languages are similar; this will also make you more marketable and valuable as an employee.

Programmers also update, repair, modify, and expand existing programs. Some, especially those working on large projects that involve many programmers, use computer-assisted software engineering (CASE) tools to automate much of the coding process. These tools free up a programmer to concentrate on writing the unique or more challenging parts of a program. Other tools include applications that increase productivity by combining compiling, code walkthrough, code generation, test data generation, and debugging functions. Programmers also use libraries of basic code that can be modified or customized for a specific application. In many cases, several programmers work together as a team under a senior programmer's supervision. It is common for new programmers to work under the supervision of senior programmers, even if they are not working on a huge project.

Programmers test a program by running it to ensure that the instructions are correct and that the program produces the desired outcome. If errors do occur, the programmer must make the appropriate change and recheck the program until it produces the correct results. This process is called testing and debugging, and may continue for as long as a program is used.

Programmers may work directly with experts from various fields to create specialized software—either programs designed for specific clients or packaged software for general use—ranging from games and educational software to programs for desktop publishing and financial planning. Programming of packaged software constitutes one of the hottest segments of the computer programming industry today.

Programmers can be grouped into one of two types: applications programmers and systems programmers. Applications programmers write programs to handle a specific task, such as a program to track inventory within an organization. They also may revise existing packaged software or customize generic applications purchased from vendors. Systems programmers, on the other hand, write programs to maintain and control computer systems software for operating systems, networked systems, and database systems. In some organizations, workers known as programmer-analysts are responsible for both systems analysis and programming.

Computer Security Specialist

This person is responsible for protecting computer systems against all forms of illegal intrusion, including viruses, data theft, fraud, and more. This can be achieved by setting up automatic security monitoring programs, reviewing system logs for evidence of tampering, and educating users about the importance of good security practices (some feel this is the hardest part of the job!), among other things. In most companies, a person in this line of works starts at the trainee or assistant level, becomes a security specialist, and then is promoted to director of information systems security. Related fields include technical writing, technical support, systems design, programming, and artificial intelligence.

Computer Systems Designer

Any computer system that is available online or in a store was carefully created and designed by a computer systems designer. These designers select each separate component—the disk drives, motherboard, video system, etc.—to put together systems designed for specific users and their needs. For example, the average home computer user will have different requirements than someone who is purchasing a "fleet" of computers for a business—a system for a home user may have a decent graphics and sound systems (since many people use their computer to play games), whereas a business user's computer may have a more powerful processor to keep up with data processing and storage demands.

People often begin in an entry-level position, are eventually promoted to a senior-level position, and then become a lead designer or move into management. Others may prefer to become a consultant for other companies. Systems designers often work closely with people in the marketing department and with programmers. Related fields include systems integration, computer hardware design and engineering, telecommunications, embedded systems design, and technical support.

Database Administrator

Database administrators work with database management systems software and determine ways to organize and store data. They identify user needs and set up new computer databases. In many cases, database administrators must integrate data from outdated systems into a new one. They also test and coordinate modifications to the system when needed and troubleshoot problems when they occur. This person ensures the performance of the system, understands the platform on which the database runs, and adds new users to the system. Because many databases are connected to the Internet, database administrators also must plan and coordinate security measures with network administrators. With the growing volume of sensitive data and the increasing interconnectedness of computer networks, data integrity, backup systems, and database security have become increasingly important aspects of the job of database administrators.

Database administrators typically begin their careers as database analysts or programmers, then move into administration, then information systems management, eventually becoming a chief information officer (CIO). Related fields include systems administration, database analysis, Internet applications programmer, and Web design.

Database Analyst

A database analyst designs and creates programs used to collect, maintain, and analyze data used by business organizations, government entities, and other institutions, and runs related reports that managers and analysts then use when making business decisions. In addition, a database analyst changes these programs to reflect changes in business practices, new standards, or new regulations. A person in this field typically starts at the trainee level, becomes an analyst, then a database administrator, and then an information systems manager. Related fields include systems analysis, Web design, and data mining.

Data Entry Operator

This position is exactly what it sounds like—entering data into a computer system. This can be data from bank statements, data for an online application, or data for an online survey. However, this job is not always as easy as it sounds. The data must be entered accurately and as error-free as possible and performed at a steady, efficient pace. People often start at an entry-level position and move up the ladder into more senior positions, perhaps becoming an office manager or the manager of a data entry department (this is more often the case with larger companies). Related fields include desktop publishing, word processing, and typesetting.

Data Miner

Data miners study databases in a wide range of areas—business, government, science—and study the information these databases contain, applying certain tools and algorithms to them and looking for patterns that can leverage these databases. For example, online stores typically recommend additional purchases based on recent selections. This is an example of data mining. Most entry-level workers start as a database analyst or junior-level specialist, becoming a data mining specialist, then a senior consultant or project leader, and then a director or executive in a laboratory or corporation, for example. Related fields include programming, bioinformatics, statistics, systems analysis, database analysis, database administrator, and artificial intelligence.

Internet Applications Programmer

An Internet applications programmer, while a programmer at heart, is focused more on developing programs that add features and functionalities to a Web site, such as animations, forms, and shopping carts. Responsibilities of an Internet applications programmer can include writing programs for Web browsers, search engines, e-commerce, chat programs, and video conferencing. Unlike traditional programmers, Internet applications programmers do not usually use languages like C++. Rather, they use languages like Java, JavaScript, or VBScript. They are also highly proficient in Hypertext Markup Language (HTML).

Internet applications programmers often work with advertising and marketing departments, and may also work with writers and editors on occasion. Related fields include Web site design, computer graphics, animation/special effects programmer, and multimedia development.

Internet Service Provider

This term refers to a business entity that provides home and business customers an account through which they access the Internet. This often includes space for a Web site, hosting, and related services. Internet service providers (ISPs) connect to the Internet through special, high-capacity phone lines and arrange connections to nearby Internet "backbones"—larger ISPs that agree to pass their traffic through. Duties include setting up accounts and providing technical support for customers, and monitoring local connections and creating alternate routes, if need be. The prospects for small to medium-sized ISPs are not great, given the larger competition presented by companies like America Online, EarthLink, Verizon, and the like. Most people in this field work for the larger companies. A person typically enters at an entry-level support position and from there goes into management or a director position. Related fields include Web site design, Internet applications programmer, and Internet advertising designer.

Lead Programmer

The importance of the lead programmer cannot be overstated. This person is absolutely critical to the success of the project. The lead programmer (as the name implies) is responsible for taking the helm and leading the technical implementation of the design of a software product. Specific duties include supervising all technical aspects of the product, including engine and tools development and debugging and technical support after the product is released; ensuring that all programmers understand the ultimate architecture and vision; delegating programming tasks, and making sure that these tasks are carried out according to schedule; and ensuring that all code is properly integrated. The salary ranges from $75,000 to $120,000.

Network/Systems Administrator

Network/systems administrators and data communications analysts, also referred to as network architects, design, test, and evaluate systems such as local area networks (LANs), wide area networks

(WANs), the Internet, intranets, and other data communications systems. Systems are configured in many ways and can range from a connection between two offices in the same building to globally distributed networks, voice mail, and e-mail systems of a multinational organization. Network/systems administrators perform network modeling, analysis, and planning, often requiring both hardware and software solutions. For example, a network may involve the installation of several pieces of hardware, such as routers and hubs, wireless adaptors, and cables, while also requiring the installation and configuration of software, such as network drivers. Analysts also may research related products and make necessary hardware and software recommendations. Systems and network administrators often become information systems managers. Related fields include systems analysis, programming, software engineer, technical support, and technical writing.

Program Manager

In terms of the computer industry, this position typically has an emphasis in software development, and a program manager is responsible for overseeing all aspects of a development project, assigns tasks, manages schedules, and coordinates efforts of developers, programmers, testers, and more. They typically work for companies that produce commercial software, and often move into upper levels of management. Projects managers often work closely with people in marketing or sales, since the successful launch of a product is often contingent upon all the pieces coming together at the right time. The typical career path for a program manager is information systems manager and then chief information officer (CIO). Related fields include systems analysis and marketing.

Quality Assurance Specialist

A quality assurance (QA) specialist is responsible for testing and evaluating software programs to make sure they work correctly and meet the required specifications. They support programmers, who are focused more on the inner workings of a program and who do not always anticipate ways in which users will actually use a program. In a sense, programmers are depending on QA specialists to find the bugs they missed. These people may also suggest ways a particular software program can be improved. QA specialists often start at a trainee level and then become a specialist. The more experienced specialists are promoted to a senior-level position. This person could be someone who has crossed over from a technical support or help-desk job. Other related fields include technical writer, tester, and user interface design.

Service Technician

Sooner or later, it happens: a hard drive crashes, a monitor no longer displays properly, or a computer in general is just not behaving the way it should. That is when the service technician comes in. Duties include (among other things) installing and testing new computers, repairing and upgrading equipment, and running diagnostic programs to determine the source of a problem. Some large companies have in-house technicians; most work for computer manufacturers or computer stores, supporting the products they sell. People who follow this career path and establish a good service record find themselves promoted to a senior-level position and perhaps eventually managing a service department. Related fields include computer hardware manufacturing technician, systems integration, technical support, and sales.

Software Engineer

Computer software engineers apply the principles of computer science and mathematical analysis to the design, development, testing, and evaluation of the software and systems that make computers work. The tasks performed by these workers change rapidly, reflecting new areas of specialization or changes in technology, as well as the unique needs of their employers.

Software engineers can be involved in the design and development of many types of software, including computer games, word processing and business applications, operating systems and network distribution, and compilers, which convert programs to machine language for execution on a computer.

Similar to systems analysts, computer software engineers begin by analyzing users' needs, and then design, test, and develop software to meet those needs. They may also take on the role of a computer programmer but not always. Computer software engineers must be experts in operating systems and middleware (software that acts as a bridge between software programs or applications) to ensure that the underlying systems will work properly.

Examples of duties a software engineer may be responsible for include tracking each department's computer needs for a company—ordering, inventory, billing, and payroll, for example—and making suggestions about the technical direction. They also might set up the organization's intranets—networks that link computers within the organization and ease communication among various departments.

People in this field often start as a software engineer or programmer or analyst, move to a lead programmer or systems analyst, then into project management, and then to managing information systems. Related fields include systems programming, database analysis, data mining, and systems integration.

Systems Analyst

A systems analyst, as the name implies, analyzes an organization's needs and designs programs to meet these needs. This includes writing the "blueprints" for the software program, choosing the most appropriate tools and methods, supervising the writing of the code, testing the program, fixing bugs, and adding requested features. Such people often work with both technical and nontechnical staff.

As a systems analyst gains experience, he or she may be promoted to senior or lead positions, or even into management positions, such as manager of information systems or chief information officer. Those who find their career leads them into a particular niche may find opportunities as independent consultants, or may choose to start their own consulting firms. Related fields include system integration, database analysis, and information systems manager.

Systems Consultant

Similar to a systems analyst, a systems consultant analyzes problems and designs appropriate solutions, with an emphasis on selecting, installing, and configuring hardware and software. Because this person is often brought in to a company on a short-term basis, they may also have a hand in training employees in the operation of a new system. Their services are typically required when a company is expanding its information processing facilities or experiencing problems integrating systems and software. Because systems consultants work in a short-term or freelance capacity, the career path is typically what such a person creates for him- or herself. Some do go on to become information systems managers at a company. Related fields include systems analysis and systems integration.

Systems Programmer

A systems programmer builds the tools that other programmers use. They design and write programs that interact with a computer's low-level operating system, such as device drivers and utilities. Some work directly on the development of operating systems; others write drivers (special programs that allow an operating system to control peripheral devices like printers and mice); still others write development aids that programmers use to write code, such as compilers and editors. In most cases, a systems programmer starts out in an entry-level position, is promoted to a senior-level position, and then becomes a lead programmer or project manager in systems development. Related fields include user interface design and systems design.

Technical Support Specialist

Help-desk technicians typically work with external users. Technical support specialists, however, are generally in-house in that they respond to inquiries from their organizations' computer users and may run automatic diagnostics programs to resolve problems. They also install, modify, clean, and repair computer hardware and software. They may write training manuals and train users in how to use new computer hardware and software. These people also oversee the daily performance of their company's computer systems and evaluate how useful software programs are. As with help-desk technicians, people in this field often start at an entry level, work up to the senior level, and then go into a management position. Related fields include testing, systems consultant, technical writer, and technical editor.

Telecommunications Technician/Engineer

These are the people responsible for physically setting up computer systems, including the cables, telephone, or fiber-optic lines used for networking and communication; troubleshooting any problems that may arise; and configuring, specifying, and monitoring the

Professional
Ethics

Maintain Neutrality

Stay out of office politics, and strive never to get caught in the middle of them. Instead, if appropriate, work to offer an open arena in which conflicting opinions can resolve their issues—or at least find a happy medium. Remember, people's emotions are often involved in these situations, especially as it pertains to their work, so listen to all sides, and if there is conflicting information—for example, one person says that a bug in a software program should be solved in one way, while another person feels it should be resolved in another way—you may be the one who needs to rationally and unemotionally decide the right path. If necessary, take the issue to someone who has the authority to resolve it. Maintain your position of neutrality. If it comes to it, be prepared to walk away.

configuration and transmission of data, among other things. When entering this field, people typically do so at the trainee or assistant level and then move up to a senior position. From there, depending on the size of the company, they may move into supervisory or managerial positions. Some go on to pursue careers in engineering. Related fields include network analysis, computer hardware technician, hardware manufacturing, and service technician.

Tester

Testers play a crucial role in the development of a software product, whether that is the newest release of an operating system, an interactive Web site, or the hottest video game. In one sense, the tester is getting paid to play around with a product; however, their primary job is to test specific features, making sure that the product works as designed. Successful testers have a keen eye for detail, good communication skills, and patience. While testers do not need to have programming knowledge, it certainly does not hurt to understand how a particular piece of software works and all the things that can go wrong with it.

User Interface Designer

This person designs the menus, icons, graphics, and other features that people use when interacting with a computer program or operating system (called a graphical user interface, or GUI). When carrying out this task, a user interface designer looks to make the interface components intuitive, consistent, and not awkward. For example, it makes sense to use an icon that looks like a trash can to indicate where to send a deleted folder, or a pencil icon to indicate a word-processing program. In addition, components and techniques should be the same across applications in a suite (cutting and pasting, for example, should be the same in Microsoft Word as it is in Microsoft Excel).

In most cases, people in this field start at the trainee level, become an actual user interface designer, than a lead designer, and then a manager. Related fields include technical writing, systems analysis, systems programming and integration, and multimedia.

Webmaster

To be sure, Web site designers can play a role in maintaining and updating a Web site, but that type of oversight often falls to the Webmaster. This person may oversee writers and programmers who provide content for the site, monitors the site's performance, and ensures its security. Webmasters typically begin their career as a Web site designer, then go into applications programming, eventually becoming a Webmaster. In smaller companies, this job may just be one of many the default "techie" is responsible for. In a larger company, however, a dedicated Webmaster is required. Related fields include Internet applications programmer, systems/network administration, and multimedia.

Web Producer

This position is really a cross between a writer, an editor, and a marketer. Web producers are responsible for driving traffic to a Web site; thus, one of the primary tasks for a person in this position is to always consider the user experience. They need to determine, for example, the best way in which content should appear on a page—should it be in article form, slide show form, or video form? The extent to which a Web producer is responsible for making decisions related to content varies—some have more authority than others.

Most Web producers start out as writers or designers—no specific degree is necessary, but a person interested in this position should have at least a college degree and preferably some experience running Web sites. Relevant skills include writing and marketing, as well as some knowledge of HTML and Flash programming. Such people also need to be familiar with tracking and interpreting metrics related to Internet use and Web site traffic.

Web Site Designer

A Web designer—also called a Web programmer, Web developer, Internet or intranet developer, or Webmaster— is responsible for day-to-day Web site creation and design. Web designers combine the skills of a computer programmer with those of a graphic designer. They work with all of the elements of a Web site—text, images, graphics, and more—to come up with functional, interesting, and user-friendly designs.

Because this is still a relatively new position as far as computer technology goes, there is no real path for advancement, per se. As with consultants, this position often evolves into whatever the motivated person wants it to be. As skills grow, so, too, can responsibilities. There can be crossover between Web site design and applications programming, so a person who is looking to advance his or her career as a Web site designer would do well to acquire knowledge of programming. Other related fields include systems/network administrator, multimedia developer, technical writing, and technical editing.

Web Site Flow Architect

Think of this role as that of a specialized Web site designer. The Web site flow architect is responsible for ensuring that a Web site not only looks attractive, but that the design is such that any user to the site can navigate through it in a number of ways with ease—in other words, the site flows well! This is often a natural next step for a graphic designer or user interface designer. From here, a site flow architect may go on to become a Web producer or product development manager. Advancement prospects are good, with salaries ranging from $45,000 to $95,000. An undergraduate degree in computer engineering, graphic design, or industrial design is essential, as is experience in software development and functional design.

Nontechnical Jobs

The jobs in this section are more managerial in nature. They tend to be held by people who started out in an entry-level capacity, who have a solid grounding in technology, and moved up the career ladder to end up in one of these positions.

Account Manager

This position may also be known as an "advertising and promotions manager." More than just a salesperson, in the B2B world, the account manager is responsible for one or more customers in a specific segment of a market. For many online companies, this position involves combining traditional marketing skills with hosting and automation platforms to not only target the right audience for a product or service, but also reach them; generate maximum demand for the product or service; cultivate relationships with prospective clients; and qualify and deliver leads to the sales department.

Assistant Producer

This is the lowest level of the production ladder. Some people move to the production area from testing or development. The assistant producer supports the associate producer and other producers as necessary. Possible duties include shipping and receiving documents, equipment, and CDs to developers; making backups of all project material; testing milestone deliveries; assisting with testing; and assisting with product design, among other things.

Associate Producer

Despite the subordinate-sounding word *associate*, the associate producer has a critical role in the production team. As the producer's go-to person, the associate producer steps in and handles anything the producer is not able to tackle, especially when it comes to internal team-related issues. A sampling of tasks the associate producer is responsible for include: assisting the producer in budgeting and scheduling, tracking the development team's progress, helping the producer to maintain project documentation, overseeing assistant producers, attending trade shows and conferences, and running focus tests.

Director of Marketing Research

Also known as a marketing director or marketing manager, this person is responsible for a myriad of tasks, including the development of marketing strategies, identification of potential consumers, and development of new products. This is a high-stress position, with long hours, but the money might be worth it to some people. According to the U.S. Bureau of Labor Statistics, the median national salary for a marketing manager is in the range of $80,000 to start and can go as high as $150,000. While some employers prefer potential workers to have earned a bachelor's or master's degree in business administration with an emphasis on marketing, additional courses in economics, accounting, business law, finance, mathematics, and statistics may help. In highly technical Internet-related industries, such as computer and electronics manufacturing, bachelor's degrees in engineering or science, combined with master's degrees in business administration, may be preferred.

Director of Operations

While the exact nature of this position varies from company to company, in general, the director of operations oversees the day-to-day activities of an organization, usually with a focus on the systems and procedures required to accomplish the company's mission and goals in the marketplace. Specific duties could include supervising personnel, purchasing, research and development, manufacturing, marketing and sales departments. This person often reports to the chief operations officer (COO). A master's degree in business administration is a typical educational background for directors of operations, but a person typically spends many years working up through several levels of corporate hierarchy before assuming a role like this one.

Executive Producer

An executive producer typically oversees a line of products. There is little creative involvement with the actual product at this position, although executive producers are expected to still keep in touch with the "real world," so to speak, by testing the product and reporting any comments and feedback. This is definitely not an entry-level position. Sample duties of an executive producer include maintaining

connections with marketing, sales, PR, and legal departments; negotiating development contract and license agreements; and creating
the company's product plan.

Industry Analyst

People who are able to follow—and perhaps even anticipate—trends
in Internet-related industries are valuable indeed, as in any field.
Because this particular field changes so fast, however, people who
have special insight and who can analyze performance among companies may find themselves of special importance to those working
in product development or marketing. Analysts compile information on both the big picture and the little picture: How are specific
companies doing? What effect is that having on the industry as a
whole? What sectors or particular stocks should a company invest
in? Where are the problem areas, and what companies or trends
should be avoided? It is the job of the analyst to answer these and
other questions. Some work in-house for companies, some work for
business publications, and others work in the investment industry.
Analysts often work with marketing and accounting departments,
as well as with upper-level managers. When working for a particular company, a person typically starts at the assistant level, works
up to a senior-level position, and perhaps becomes a manager of an
investment research group. People who are deemed to have particular valuable knowledge—the pundit—may even find themselves a
regular guest on news programs. Related fields include marketing,
journalism, and public relations.

Information Systems Auditor

Auditors of electronic data processing (EDP) keep a close eye on data
processing applications, looking for errors and mistakes—both acci-
dental and cases of fraud. These people may also be responsible for
ensuring that the companies they work for adhere to certain government regulations and industry standards. Such jobs are often in high
demand in industries such as banking, insurance, and accounting,
where there is a large amount of financial data and its proper handling
must be safeguarded. People in this field typically start at a trainee- or
entry-level position and are promoted through the ranks, eventually
reaching a senior-level position. Some go on to become a partner at

a public accounting firm, become freelance consultants, or manage an auditing department in a company. Related fields include systems analyst, certified public accountant (CPA), and computer security.

Information Systems Director

This is the person in charge of planning for and supervising all information systems departments in an organization. This includes developing IT-related budgets, expansion plans, strategic plans, and more. They often work with managers in other departments to set organization-wide standards with regard to equipment, training, and other practices, as well as to devise ways of using computer technology to provide better service and better meet the company's goals. People in this position typically start as a systems administrator, become a low-level manager in a related departed (such as data processing), and then become a director of information systems. In small- to medium-sized companies, this position may be at the top level. In larger companies, an information systems director may go on to become chief information officer. Related fields include systems administration, computer operations, technical support, and management.

Information Systems Manager

This position is often one step below that of information systems director at many companies. Duties typically include overseeing all aspects of information technology operation, such as technical support, training, network administration, and database operations. They may work for universities, government offices, or small to medium-sized companies. Specific responsibilities may include supervising system administrators, preparing operating budgets, and planning for the upgrading or expansion of software. Information systems managers often work with managers in other departments to ensure appropriate and efficient use of computer resources and to make sure users' needs and questions are met. People in this position typically start as a systems administrator or support manager or support technician. From here, an information systems manager can move into a director position or even chief information officer. Related fields include systems administrator, systems analyst, and systems consultant.

Localization Manager

Localization is the process of configuring a product so that it can be sold in another country. This involves changing the text and language—and sometimes the code and graphics as well (from a vertical to horizontal orientation, for example)—to the language of the destination country (or countries). The localization manager is the production person in charge of this process (salaries range from $30,000 to $50,000). Localization can be a difficult task, because it encompasses so many different things, from installers and menu selections, to help files and hints, and even the code in which the product is written and the platform it is designed for.

Marketing Specialist

Just as with any field, people who choose to focus on marketing become a knowledgeable expert in a given domain—this can include everything from software to hardware and anything in between. Marketing specialists study this industry, identifying possible new markets; create brochures and other display material; perform demonstrations at trade shows and conferences; and use surveys, focus groups, and other forms of feedback to determine if customers' needs are being met and how a product or service can be improved. People generally enter this field as an assistant, become a specialist or focus on research, then become an assistant marketing manager or product manager, before becoming the manager of a marketing department. Related fields include project management, research, and consulting.

Product Development Manager

Product development managers are responsible for ensuring that a company's products do not become outdated or unmarketable. As far as Internet-related jobs go, product development managers may be responsible for travel packages, software products, and more. This person is also responsible for finding marketing opportunities and taking advantage of them. People in this position must have skills and understanding in marketing research, sales forecasting, and promotional planning. Their mission is to successfully take a product from concept to commercialization. This is often a common career move for people who start their careers in marketing and advertising or sales.

Software Applications Trainer

People who have an in-depth understanding of certain software programs may find it rewarding to teach others. Trainers usually offer classes in specific programs or operating systems, and can work within corporations, community colleges, vocational schools, employment agencies, adult education, or continuing education centers. Such positions are often in constant demand—software is always being updated and workers need retraining when previous skills fall by the wayside. People typically enter this field as a basic or entry-level instructor. As they gain experience, they often advance to become a senior-level trainer, a manager in charge of other trainers, or an independent consultant, offering advanced or specialized workshops. Related positions include technical writing, technical support, and management.

Like industry analysts, statisticians also analyze data and draw conclusions from it. Unlike analysts, however, statisticians focus on mathematical data, using it to create computer simulations, which can then be compared to real-world scenarios. People entering this field typically start as an assistant. As they gain experience, they can be promoted to a senior level, and may even become director of a statistical research department or move into academia. Related fields include accounting, database analysis, data mining, engineering, programming, and marketing.

Systems Integrator

This person is responsible for combining various hardware and software components into a system that best meets a particular client's needs (typically, these clients are large companies with anywhere from dozens to hundred of users). A systems integrator achieves this task by becoming familiar with the company—the physical location, what kind of business the company is engaged in, and how it carries out this business. Once the recommendations have been made and approved, the systems integrator oversees its installation, which can include training workers (if needed), and monitoring the system to fix any problems or issues that come up. People entering this field may start in a company and eventually become an independent consultant, or they may start as a technical assistant, gain experience as a systems integrator, and then become a systems engineer. Related fields include systems analysis and sales.

Technical Director

Technical directors are often used when a software product is being developed externally. Because producers do not usually have the technical expertise to judge the quality of programming by themselves, the technical director steps in and checks the development team's code to make sure that it meets certain software engineering standards. This position is also known as a technical advisor or technical producer. Other responsibilities of a technical director include tracking down and solving particularly difficult bugs and other technical problems, obtaining coding resources and tools for the team, and examining the proposed technical design of a product to determine if it is worth the publisher's efforts.

Problem
Solving

Testing, Testing

There are two opposing priorities with Internet products: the need for quick-paced releases and the expectation of reliability. With enterprise software, there may be three to six months to test the product with a small set of customers in beta before making a wide release. With B2C Internet products, an incremental new feature might be released every three days or so. There just is not the same time frame for testing, so people have to work fast and hard. With B2C Internet products, failure can be instantaneous and catastrophic. A small change that introduces a bug in how a logon might work for a Web site may prevent all members from logging into the system—and all revenue comes to a halt immediately. Think of the consequences for a moment, if this happened to a company like Amazon or eBay.

In addition, not all browsers are the same, yet a product is expected to work the same on every single one of them and on every version. What works on Internet Explorer version 8 may not work on version 6, but customers do not care—they just want (and expect) the product to work. Thus, it takes a great deal more testing on different environments than people may expect, given the theoretically "standardized" Internet.

This is an advisory position, not a managerial one, although the technical director will verify certain project milestones with respect to code and authorize whether work should continue to the next phase (and if payment should be disbursed!). This also is not an entry-level position. Successful candidates must demonstrate proven programming experience, have extensive technical knowledge, and have years of experience working with software development teams.

Technical Support Manager

This person may oversee either a help-desk department or an internal technical support department. Duties typically include hiring and training support technicians, coordinating shift schedules, assembling and organizing support documentation (such as manuals or databases), and providing supplementary support or resolving escalated situations. Technical support managers often work with engineers, program developers, and technical writers to resolve problems with a software program or to improve its usability. People in this field typically have moved up the ranks to become a senior technical support representative or a shift manager at a help desk. From a management position, they may advance to a director of technical support, depending on the size of the organization. Related fields include technical editing, technical writing, information systems manager, and systems administration.

Management-Level Jobs

The jobs in this section are held by those at the top of the career ladder. In some cases, these people started at the bottom and worked their way to the top. However, many an Internet entrepreneur is the CFO, CTO, and CIO of his or her company—as well as the database technician, technical support person, and general office support staff.

Business/Legal Affairs Manager

This department deals with contracts, licenses, and other legal matters. Often composed of lawyers, this team may also include people with experience in product or company acquisitions. Companies who produce video games, for example, require contracts relating to all sorts of things—permissions, nondisclosure agreements, recording contracts, licensing agreements, contracts with vendors and distributors—and the business/legal affairs department makes sure that all the t's are crossed and all the i's are dotted.

Chief Executive Officer (CEO)

This is the person responsible for the overall health of the company and—whether for good or ill—is often associated with the image of the company. Some CEOs are very hands-on, preferring to know what is going on with all areas of the company. Others are more hands-off, preferring to let the people they hired carry out the jobs they are supposed to do. And while the CEO may not have any direct experience with computers or software or video games or anything Internet-related, this person knows enough to hire people who do.

Chief Financial Officer (CFO)

It costs a lot of money to produce software—and even hardware, for that matter. For starters, there are the people you need to hire: talented people who know what their skills are worth. Then there are the cutting-edge tools and technology your company may need so that you can produce a state-of-the-art product. Marketing and licenses cost money, too. Throw in the general overhead of running a business—rent, utilities, office supplies, and so on—and it is no surprise that it takes an enormous amount of capital to fund most any high-tech company these days and keep it viable. The person that task falls to is the CFO. This person typically has a background in accounting, and has a proven track record with other companies. However, this person also is not afraid to take a calculated risk when necessary in order to see potentially monumental gains.

Chief Information Officer

This is typically the highest-ranking information services executive in a company. This person is responsible for long-term planning and organization-wide policy with respect to all computer-related activities. They often present proposals to the chief executive officer (CEO) or to a corporation's board of directors. A CIO pays attention to how their competitors are using technology and how their company can use it better. Since this is a top-level executive position, any moves from here are typically in a lateral direction, such as chief executive officer or vice president for research or planning.

Chief Technology Officer

This position is similar in duties and scope to a chief information officer and is a high-level position responsible for leveraging monetary, intellectual, or political capital into technology to further a company's objectives or goals. They often oversee technical staff, particularly those engaged in the development of new technologies or in software development. Whereas a chief information officer is focused on solving problems or meeting the company's goals by using existing technology, the chief technology officer is looking to achieve these same things by developing new technologies. As with a CIO, this is a top-level executive position, so career moves will go in a lateral rather than vertical direction.

Chapter 4

Tips for Success

Now that you have begun a career in the Internet field, how do you keep it going? Where should it go from here? Recent and emerging trends may have an effect on a person's career, causing it to go in a different direction. As has been stressed repeatedly throughout this book, the Internet is constantly evolving and spawning new technologies, new jobs, and new career paths.

This chapter will provide helpful guidance on how to best advance this career and keep it moving in a desired direction. Where relevant, certifications and degrees that can move your career forward will be addressed (some fields, like programming or design, require a degree for a career to get anywhere; an Internet entrepreneur or a writer may be able to get along just fine without any formal training). In addition, because the career path a person starts out on is not necessarily the one that they continue down, this chapter will offer advice on where to find that next job and how to land an interview.

The Internet is a hotbed of passion, vision, creativity, openness—and risk. An understanding of the culture it has brought into being can go a long way in understanding how best to drive a career forward.

Reputation Is Everything

Whether you work for a large company or are a sole proprietor running an online business, professionalism is everything—a lack of it can make or break your career. And it is not a hard thing to do. A lot of it goes back to those golden rules learned in kindergarten: Treat everyone with respect, and if you cannot say anything nice, do not say anything at all. Another important aspect of establishing a professional reputation is to be aware of your limitations, while striving to go beyond them. For example, a technical writer may have an interest in project management (a common career move for many writers); however, that does not necessarily mean that this person has the skills and experience to take on a huge content management project right off the bat. There is a huge difference between writing or editing content and managing a team of writers, developers, and others in order to get that content to users. Perhaps this writer needs to brush up on his or her organizational and time management skills, or mentor with an already experienced project manager, taking on some of the less important tasks while learning the ins and outs of project management. There is nothing wrong with wanting to expand one's skill set—in fact, it is a trait that many employers often look for. The key is to formulate a plan for doing so and seeking out people who can help you hone the skills you need. It is arrogant to think you can do everything—and that arrogance can quickly tarnish a reputation.

Honesty and accountability go a long way in establishing a professional reputation. If you did not do a good job on something, be honest about it. Trying to blame someone else for problems you encountered or as an excuse for the state of your work, or just producing work of low quality when you (and perhaps your boss) knows you are capable of more, will be noticed and remembered when it comes to promotions. Attention to detail is just as important when it comes to one's professional reputation as it is for many positions in general.

Another one of the quickest ways you can ruin your professional reputation is by using negative comments. Avoid words like "do not," "won't," and "can't." For example, rather than saying "I do not work well with negative people," say, "I find working with negative people an enjoyable challenge, although it can be tough and I would like to avoid it if possible." The first statement implies that you are not adaptable and are unable to work with a variety of people. The latter statement shows that you are flexible and willing to tackle difficult situations.

Want to kill a professional reputation fast? Have people think you are unreliable or picky about the type of work you are willing to do.

For example, rather than saying that you "do not" do project management, say you "did not" do project management in your last job but would be willing to try it with guidance where needed. This goes back to recognizing limitations, yet being willing to move beyond them. You may find that you actually hate project management and are not very good at it. At least the attempt was made and a willingness to try something new was demonstrated. Be a person who does things and gets things done. Be proactive—look for what needs to be done and be prepared to do whatever it takes to help. Work that you are responsible for should be the highest quality and should be completed on time.

How Social Media Affects Reputation

According to a 2009 poll by Forrester Research, 75 percent of Internet users participate in some form of social networking, up from 56 percent in October 2008. The advent (and explosion) in the use of social networking sites like LinkedIn and Facebook can also be used to establish a professional reputation, especially for many people who have decided to use the Internet to set up an online business. While it is practically a requirement that any business looking to achieve any measure of success set up a page on Facebook, given the huge amounts of traffic these sites see on a daily basis, Holly Berkley, author of *Marketing in the New Media*, explains that these sites are not always the most advantageous for a business. She recommends that people take the time to find the social networking sites that are most popular with the business's target audience and make sense for the particular product or brand. For example, a clothing company may choose to promote and market its products through FabSugar. com or ShopStyle.com in addition to a Facebook page since the first two sites are more likely to attract their target audience, whereas the Facebook page may not. Some companies find that online blogs are the most successful approach to marketing and reaching out to that target audience, especially when relationships with key bloggers can be established.

The Value of Social Networks

That being said, the importance of Facebook cannot be ignored as a promotion and reputation-building tool. If you are a sole proprietor with an Internet-based business, Danielle Babb, author of *The Online*

Professor's Guide to Starting an Internet Business, offers the following advice with regard to what to do on sites like Facebook—and what to avoid. She stresses the importance of not being someone different on these sites than who you are in your business. The two are intertwined, like it or not, and social networking should be used to build a brand. Maintain the business's appeal, Babb says, and avoid issues where the business could lose the trust of its customers (or potential customers). She also stresses the importance of separating business from pleasure—do not link your business's page with a personal page. Allowing visitors to your site to see photos of your last vacation to Vegas can quickly tarnish the image you want your customers to have of your company and you as the face behind it.

How to Get Ahead

The number of careers that the Internet has given birth to is vast. There may very well be jobs out there that no one has even thought of it yet. After all, even 15 years ago no one knew what a database administrator, Web master, or systems manager was. This chapter cannot possibly cover every career path and the requirements in each. Because more concrete, easily defined professions—particularly those in fields like computers, programming, writing, marketing, and sales—have more obvious requirements when it comes to training and certification, those will be discussed here. Readers are encouraged to refer to Chapter 6 for more specific information on other areas. That chapter provides an extensive list of associations and organizations that often have details on how to network and advance one's career.

Microsoft Certifications

Certifications are available for nearly every Microsoft application or technology and are useful for a wide range of computer careers, including IT professionals, developers, office workers, home users, and technology trainers. In case you are thinking that certification will not help you advance your career, consider this. According to a survey conducted by Microsoft, 66 percent of managers believe that certifications improve the level of service offered to end users and consumers, and 75 percent believe that certifications are important to team performance. So what certifications does Microsoft offer? Five different levels are available:

→ Desktop Support Series
→ Technology Series
→ Professional Series
→ Master Series
→ Architect Series

The Desktop Support series validates desktop computer skills for the 2007 Microsoft Office System and other versions of Microsoft Office, along with the Windows Vista operating system. Certifications in this series demonstrate advanced, cross-industry and cross-job capabilities, such as managing budgets and presentations, and supporting organizations. Two certifications are available: Microsoft Certified Application Specialist (MCAS) and Microsoft Office Specialist (MOS).

The Technology Series is designed to validate a person's ability to implement, build, troubleshoot, and debug a particular Microsoft technology, such as Windows Server, Microsoft .NET Framework, or Microsoft SQL Server. In order to earn a particular certification, a person must pass anywhere from one to three exams and have at least one year of relevant experience. A person who earns a certification is considered a Microsoft Certified Technology Specialist (MCTS) and more than 30 certifications are currently available.

The Professional Series certification validates a comprehensive set of job-related skills, such as project management, system design, operations management, and planning. Employers often consider such a certification a reliable indicator of on-the-job-performance. In order to earn this certification, a person must pass anywhere from one to three exams and have one or more technology (MCTS) certifications. Two certifications are available, based on job roles: Microsoft Certified IT Professional and Microsoft Certified Professional Developer.

A Master Series certification demonstrates a person can successfully design and implement solutions that solve highly complex business challenges. The certifications focus on specific technologies, such as Microsoft Exchange Server 2007, Windows Server 2008–Directory, and Microsoft Office SharePoint Server 2007. The courses provide expert-level classroom training and labs that incorporate real-world customer scenarios and include both computer- and lab-based exams. The instructors are Microsoft experts and Microsoft global network partners who are experts in their disciplines.

The Architect Series also provides classroom training and labs based on real-world scenarios. A person who earns certification as a Microsoft Certified Architect (MCA) is considered an industry expert in IT architecture. To obtain this certification, applicants must definitively demonstrate seven competencies of business acumen and technological proficiency during a Review Board interview with a panel of industry experts. Two different certification tracks are available: MCA Technology and MCA Infrastructure.

Other Certifications

For database administrators, certification in two languages in particular can give someone an edge in advancing their career: SQL and Oracle. Various organizations and schools offer such tests. Typically, such tests demonstrate a person's proficiency in implementing and maintaining databases using specific instructions and specifications.

Keeping
in Touch

Networking

Networking can be vital to your career, and it is not complicated—at least, it does not need to be. Take every opportunity to meet new people who share your professional interests. Join a professional organization in your field (see Chapter 6 for an extensive list of associations and organizations), and keep in touch with your alumni association. Today, many jobs are found through networking rather than through traditional methods, such as online job boards and company Web sites. Create a professional online presence and maintain it. Set up a profile on LinkedIn, the leading online professional network, and start linking to professionals you know—your friends and family members, alumni, and former co-workers. The key aspect to keep in mind, however, is to always be professional and think carefully about what you post. Employers often search these sites when recruiting. Take care that you do not post any disparaging information that can come back later and possibly prevent you from being considered for a position.

A thorough knowledge of the product (SQL or Oracle) is demonstrated, along with an understanding of how to use available tools and how to explore the user interface. These are not the only languages in which certification is available. Nearly every language or profession mentioned in this book offers certification at differing levels. Chapter 6 provides information to get you started.

Certifications are available for Web designers as well, starting with basic certification and getting progressively more complex. CIW, the Certified Internet Web Professional program, offers an Associate certification, referred to as the Foundations exam. It demonstrates a person's proficiency with Internet technology, page authoring, and networking basics.

Another basic certification is the Certified Web Designer (CWD) certification. This was offered by the Association of Web Professionals (AWP). However, that organization is no longer in existence. Fortunately, Jupiter Systems purchased the contents and intellectual property rights to this exam and has continued the certification tests. The exam, which is online, demonstrates proficiency in basic Internet technology and Web design skills. Web Manager and Technician Certifications are also available.

WebYoda's Online Webmaster (WOW) Academy is "committed to offering the best Webmaster training courses, assessment exams, and certification options to meet the needs of aspiring Web professionals." To that end, they offer a CAW (Certified Associate Webmaster) certification. Successful completion of certification demonstrates basic proficiency in the following areas:

- Internet Basics
- Markup and Scripting
- Web Graphics
- Web Multimedia
- Web Site Design
- Web Site Management
- Legal Issues
- Web Accessibility
- Web Project Management
- Web Business Management
- Web Marketing

The World Wide Web Consortium (WC3) is the group that sets the standards for the Internet. They offer a basic 70-question exam that results in an HTML Developer Certificate and tests applicants on HTML, XHTML, and Cascading Style Sheet (CSS).

Brainbench offers several certification preparation exams. Several of the skills-related exams can be combined to earn the Brainbench Certified Internet Professional (BCIP) certification.

From there, intermediate-level Web design certifications are available to the aspiring Web developer. Knowledge of coding and scripting, along with relevant job experience, is necessary in order to earn the certifications discussed next. The Associate Webmaster Professional (AWP) exam is also offered by WebYoda. Topics cover Internet fundamentals, basic and advanced HTML and XHTML knowledge, and expertise with CSS. Those who have more experience with programming languages and one year of working with ColdFusion may wish to pursue this exam. ColdFusion is an application server and software language used for Internet application development, such as for dynamic Web sites.

Web designers who are proficient in Dreamweaver who also have experience with coding, graphics, and Web site management may want to consider earning a Dreamweaver MX Certification. Dreamweaver is a Web development application that hides the HTML code details of pages from users, which makes it an ideal application for people who do not have a lot of coding experience to create web pages and sites. The Dreamweaver MX Certification, however, demonstrates a thorough understanding of the Dreamweaver application, Web page design, Web page authoring, and supporting technologies.

Adobe Flash (previously called Macromedia Flash) is a multimedia platform created by Macromedia and currently developed and distributed by Adobe Systems. It is commonly used to create animation, advertisements, and various Web page components; to integrate video into Web pages; and more recently, to develop rich Internet applications. Macromedia offers two tracks for the Flash certification: Flash MX Designer and Flash MX Developer. The Designer exam requires knowledge of Flash motion design, optimization, and publishing. The Developer exam requires knowledge of relational database design, along with one to two years of experience in software development and Web design.

Advanced Web design certifications will require a mastery of skills and technologies that go well beyond Internet and design concepts.

software, classes or other training, and magazine sub-scriptions. With regard to payment, some businesses at this level choose to process payments manually; others choose to accept credit card payments.

➔ **Level 3:** Storefront selection and payment automation. This model is more common with online-only business, but businesses that also have a brick-and-mortar store-front will make use of it too. Sweeney defines this level as "encompassing the use of an online standalone storefront, but the back end is not integrated with other systems in the business." The primary difference between this level and the previous one is that the ability to process transactions over a secure connection and in real time is extremely important. According to Sweeney, "because company systems are not integrated, businesses that choose to use this strategy have to constantly monitor inventory levels and ensure there is adequate supply, must remove out-of-stock items from the site, or need to see that an appropriate message to that effect is displayed." An example of this type of business could include a pet supply company or a company that sold beauty supplies and products.

➔ **Level 4:** Total integration. This is the most complex level of e-business and is exactly what it sounds like—both front-end and back-end systems are integrated. In other words, "inventory, accounts receivable, accounting, spe-cial offers and discounts, consumer database, customer service—everything—is completely integrated with one another, enabling the business to run like a well-oiled machine." The best example of this type of business is Amazon. The costs to set up and manage this level of e-business can be large, but the advantages are many. For example, according to Sweeney, this model makes things easier on the consumer. By asking them to create an account online, accessed with a user name and password, consumers can log on to the site and purchase items without having to enter shipping and payment informa-tion again every single time. In addition, by integrating purchase information with a customer database, spe-cific offers can be sent to select customers. (Think of the

recommendations Amazon offers based on items customers browse or buy.) Finally, integrating inventory management and the online storefront allows the storefront
to be updated automatically, so customers know immediately whether an item is in stock or not.

What Is Involved with Setup?

Once the type of e-business has been determined, it needs to be
made legal and certain paperwork needs to be filed. The requirements will vary from state to state, but at a minimum, a person will
need to get a business license, whether as a sole proprietor, a part-
nership, a limited liability corporation or limited liability partner-
ship, or a corporation. A full explanation of each of these types and
their advantages and disadvantages is beyond the scope of this book
The best thing to do is consult an accountant or attorney who can
provide advice in this matter.

If the business is going to be something other than your name—
say, Fantastic Flowers—make sure that the name is not already taken
before your register your business. This applies to the domain name
as well. A quick search online can tell you whether this is the case. In
addition, if possible, it is best to use ".com" with your domain name,
but you may want to register ".org" or ".net" as well for two reasons:
It will enable people to find your site, regardless of the suffix they
use, and it prevents someone else from hijacking your domain name
and using it to either promote their own business or tarnish yours. A
prime example of this is the difference between http://www.white-
house.gov and http://www.whitehouse.com. And when it comes to
the domain name, think about how it will look (or sound).

Once the business has been registered properly and the domain
name secured, it is time to find a Web host and someone who can
design the site (this person may be you, if you have the necessary
skills). Several types of hosting are available, including shared (one
of the most common types for new businesses because it is so afford-
able), reseller hosting, semidedicated hosting, and dedicated hosting.
They differ with regard to complexity, cost, disk space and bandwidth available, and other features. A search on Google for "best
Web hosts" is a good place to begin the search.

Other things to consider, as discussed in the previous section, are
what methods of payment you will take (if you will accept payments

online), what features the site will offer, what kind of advertising will take place (both offline and online), and whether to join an affiliate program like Google's AdWords. Also, do not forget to set up a checking account for the business. You may also need to write up a business plan or a proposal to send to investors. Again, because there are so many variables in this endeavor, it is best to check with an accountant or attorney for advice—or at least turn to one of the sources listed in Chapter 6.

Fast Facts

LinkedIn

According to the About Us page on the LinkedIn Web site, this organization has more than 39 million members in over 200 countries and territories around the world. In addition, a new member joins LinkedIn approximately every second, and about half of the organizations members are outside the United States.

But What about Marketing?

According to Holly Berkley, author of *Marketing in the New Media*, the Internet (and related technology, such as digital video recording) has changed forever the face of advertising. People now have the option to skip ads altogether and businesses, both large and small, have had to learn to adapt and think strategically about how to incorporate marketing messages into content that people want to see. This section focuses specifically on online marketing, which Berkley defines as "communicating with customers via e-mail, message boards, chat rooms, and blogs . . . updating a Web site with important product information and offers . . . any kind of promotion a company does using the Internet." In fact, Berkley believes that a business's Web site is the key to effective online marketing and how the site is designed can often make the difference in whether a business succeeds or fails.

Berkley's book offers a thorough exploration of what she calls "new media marketing," and the serious Internet entrepreneur would be well advised to check it out. Here, however, are a few of her tips:

→ **Combine traditional ads with purchased keywords** for maximum impact, and maximize the effectiveness of keyword phrases.

➡ **Use every opportunity to generate buzz for the company.** This includes ringtones, wallpaper, music downloads, DVDs, blogs, message boards, and other interactive content. Encourage customers to provide feedback on products and services for others to see.

➡ **Do not let visitors to your site ignore the advertising.** Most everyone is familiar with this tactic. How many times have you gone to a site to watch a news clip or an episode of your favorite show, but been forced to watch a 30-second ad for a car company or an insurance company first?

This book has repeatedly stressed the importance of social networking, which has become a core component of successful online advertising. YouTube, Facebook, Twitter, MySpace, LinkedIn, and Digg can all be used to help leverage a company's brand and services or products. Berkley believes blogs are important to a business for two primary reasons. First, they allow a business to develop a closer connection with customers, generate feedback, and provide customer support. Second, they are a great way to help increase search engine rankings. According to Berkley, "because blogs are largely text-based, they are easy for search engines to index. And because every entry includes a date and search engines look to post the most recently updated site first, a company's blog has a good chance of ranking high."

Take advantage of mobile marketing—delivering ads to customers and potential customers through text messages sent to cell phones and other wireless devices. Mobile marketing can be a highly effective way to strengthen a company's brand, communicate with customers, and generate a buzz about certain products or services. This is also beginning to include apps for Apple's iPhone. As of this writing, the auto insurance company GEICO, for example, began advertising its app for the iPhone that enables customers to pay their bill through the iPhone, gather information at an accident, and watch videos featuring the Gecko.

Make sure the marketing message is relevant to your audience. This one might seem obvious, but Berkley explains: "With the birth of new technologies that put customers in control, allowing them to skip past advertisements . . . the most obvious way to get consumers' attention . . . is to talk about something that is relevant or interesting to them . . . [whether] an interesting new idea or an entertaining concept."

Another marketing tactic that might seem obvious and yet is often overlooked is to clearly define and know the target audience a business is trying to reach. For example, a company likely would not target banners ads for diapers on a site for online gamers. Television ads for weight loss plans like Nutrisystem, for example, often appear during shows that women are more likely to be watching. When they do appear on shows that men are more likely to watch, the spokesperson is not a former actress, but a former sports star. Berkley advises people to answer the following questions when considering their business's target audience:

➡ What age group is being targeted?
➡ Is the audience primarily female or male?
➡ What is the targeted audience's household income?
➡ How computer-literate is the target audience?
➡ Is the target audience more likely to access the company's site at home or at work?
➡ Is the target audience more likely to have a high-speed or a dial-up connection?
➡ What hobbies does the target audience pursue?
➡ In what part of the country (or what country) is the target audience primarily located?
➡ Are most members of the target audience single or married? Do they have children?
➡ What is the average education level of the target audience?

By answering these questions, a company can market its goods and services more effectively so that the content and design of the Web site will have the most appeal possible. According to Berkley, "the number one advantage of marketing online is that the Internet allows [businesses] to reach extremely targeted audiences," so the more a company knows about its customers, the more likely they are to have a successful advertising campaign. A great way to find answers to the questions listed above, Berkley says, is to give away a product or coupon in exchange for customers sharing their demographic information.

Do not overestimate the importance of consumer-generated media. Word of mouth is no less important now than it was in the early days of advertising simply because it has moved online. In fact, according to Berkley, "with the ease of forwarding an e-mail, uploading a comment, or sending a text message, consumer feedback in today's world can be absolutely viral." She advises businesses to not only understand the reach and technology involved in consumer-generated media, but to also actually take part in it through blogs, content optimized for search engines, and, if necessary, public relations strategies. The more positive material that can be strategically placed, the more likely the positive will be seen ahead of the negative.

Make sure the company's content is user-friendly. Berkley offers the following tips in this regard:

- ➡ **Get to the point.** New visitors should be able to find out exactly what a company or product can do for them in less than 15 seconds. Everything on the home page should help a new customer make the decision intended, whether that is buying a product or service or filling out a form for more information or a quote.

- ➡ **Showcase new information and products on the home page.** Include dates and make sure the information is always located on the same place on the page. Use the site to test new promotions before releasing them in a wider (potentially more expensive) scope, such as traditional mailings.

- ➡ **While the home page is important, do not focus all attention on it.** Search engines can send visitors to any page, not just the home page, so important information, special offers, and other incentives should be clear on every page. In addition, the site should be easy to navigate and visitors should be able to get to any page they want with ease.

- ➡ **Encourage "viral marketing."** Berkley urges businesses to remind visitors to refer a company's site (or product or service) to others whenever possible. This can be as simple as an "e-mail a friend this article" link or a coupon that, when e-mailed to a friend, enables both people to take advantage of a specific savings.

- ➡ **Collect e-mail addresses.** It is better to encourage visitors to share this information with the company rather than force them. As mentioned earlier, combining a database with purchase history and information enables a company to market its products and services more

INTERVIEW

Change Is the One Constant

Edward McKillop
Technical Writer, Microsoft, Redmond, Washington

How has the Internet changed how you do your job, both positively and negatively?
The Internet has provided a whole new area to write about. It is constantly changing in scope, which changes not only what I write about, but how I am going to write about it. For example, whether the content is online help, a video script, or print material affects how I am going to write it. There are more ways in which content can be distributed, and this affects writing style to a degree. The Internet has made me become more technically savvy, which is an essential skill. This can also be a negative, in that there are so many different tools and forms in which writing needs to happen, from blogs to internal pieces, to content management systems.

What strengths and talents do you think make someone well suited for this industry?
Technical aptitude, for one thing; also, flexibility and an enjoyment of and an ability to write about something that is constantly changing. I have stayed in the technical field because I really like the people in it and I enjoy writing about the Internet and its related technology. For the most part, people in this arena are open-minded and diverse. There is a "conversation" aspect to technical writing that I also enjoy. Someone who can write well and in this style will do well in the Internet field.

Did you enter this field with a certain career path in mind? Did you have a formal plan for success, or was it on-the-fly?

effectively, so offer visitors the option to have special offers e-mailed to them, targeted newsletters, or other items in exchange for signing up on the mailing list.

Search engine optimization (SEO), discussed elsewhere in this book, is extremely important to the success of any online business. A company may have the greatest content or offer the most amazing

How does one go about planning a career in the Internet, and how hard is it to move from one position to another?

Training and degrees are needed to move up in this field. This can be as simple as a one-year certificate from a community college. These certifications are valued for two reasons: They show that you are willing to expand your skill set and that you have "follow-through." Speaking from the perspective of a technical writer, the best way to achieve success is to find a niche and become an expert in a specific area. In a large corporation like Microsoft, learn to accommodate other writing projects within your area of expertise. For example, if I am writing help files for a Microsoft Office product, I might also agree to manage blog content on that same product. Technical writers often move to senior-level writing positions, which include managing other writers and/or editors, and often become content managers. From there, they could become team leaders or producers—the opportunities are nearly endless, especially if they stay on top of the technology. Cultivate good diplomacy skills (i.e., stay above office politics).

What is the best way to quickly establish a professional reputation? What is the easiest way to trash this reputation?

Be flexible, learn to assimilate information quickly, be organized (or learn these skills, if necessary!), get to know your subject matter experts, and—perhaps most importantly—push your ego out of the way. Be honest about mistakes, whether they are yours or someone else's, and find a professional way to resolve the issues mistakes often engender.

Things that can quickly earn you a negative reputation include making a lot of mistakes, especially technical errors (if you do not truly understand a piece of technology you are writing about or how it works, find out). As a writer, I often work with programmers, developers, and the like. These people are often emotionally attached to their technology. Someone who does not understand this and who cannot respect it and who is unable to get along with such people will not do well in this field.

products or services, but if no one ever sees the site, none of that matters. Berkeley advises businesses to consider the following when optimizing their Web site for search engines:

→ **Search engines** read text, not graphics, so Web sites with graphics-laden home pages or Flash introductions may find themselves lower down in the rankings.

➡ **Choose the right keywords.** Use what visitors are more likely to type to find your site, not what you think they should type. Programs such as WordTracker.com can help determine which keyword phrases have the highest search volume. Make sure those are the phrases included in the content of the Web site.

➡ **The more keywords you can put within text links, the better.** Search engines pay extra attention to these, so look for these opportunities and take advantage of them. For example, a company that sells toys for dogs and cats will want to use the text "Click here to see more cat-nip toys and chew toys" rather than just "Click here." In addition, always add text-based navigation to your site— "Click here to return to the home page"—rather than just an icon or button for that purpose. Berkley reminds companies that if a Web site has only graphic buttons for navigation, it will be difficult for search engines to get past the home page and rank other pages.

Another way to drive traffic to a Web site is through e-mail marketing. Because people often scan the subject lines of e-mails, quickly deciding whether to read or delete, Berkley says that the more effective subject lines are the ones whose e-mails get read. To that end, she recommends that people keep subject lines short and direct, stress the benefits to the recipient, or ask a question; they should be written in a personal style; they should tie in seasonal events or holidays if possible; and they should never use the words "free," "limited offer," "buy now," or "guaranteed" nor should they include several exclamation marks or be in all caps—nothing will cause an e-mail to be rejected by server filters as spam faster.

While on the subject of spam, U.S. businesses are required by law to comply with the CAN-SPAM Act, which sets the rules for commercial e-mail, establishes requirements for commercial messages, gives recipients the right to stop receiving e-mails, and spells out tough penalties for violations. According to the U.S. Federal Trade Commission, the Act requires companies to do the following: not to use false or misleading header information, not to use deceptive subject lines, to always identify the message as an ad, to tell recipients where the company is located, to tell recipients how to opt out of receiving future e-mails, to honor opt-out requests promptly, and to monitor what others are doing on the company's behalf. In order to ensure compliance with CAN-SPAM, Berkley recommends that when it comes to e-mail marketing companies should always be honest. They should provide valid, physical contact information; not send e-mails to people who did not request them; not buy or rent e-mail lists; always keep lists up-to-date; and always provide an opt-out option.

Obviously, some of Berkley's advice is more attainable (and suitable) for companies that have a larger advertising budget to work with, but small, emerging online businesses can certainly make use of her tips, too. At the very least, it may get you to start thinking outside the box and come up with new ways to promote your business. After all, even Amazon started out as a tiny fish in a vast Internet pond.

When It Is Time to Move On: Advice for Job Hunting and Job Interviewing

When looking for a job and launching a new career, it is important to treat this like a full-time job in itself. Take this seriously. Devote a set amount of time to job hunting every day. Author Mike Farr, who has been teaching and writing on career planning and job search techniques for 20 years, recommends that motivated career launchers consider the following steps.

Identify Your Key Skills

Your "key skills" include the ones that are actually related to the job you are seeking. For example, knowledge of Java, Perl, and C# computer languages; experience with database administration; or a stint as a computer support specialist are all practical skills relevant to a career in computers and programming. Job-related skills such as these are often (but not always) in line with the path on which you plan to launch your career.

Regardless of the field, there are certain skills that most employers look for in an applicant, such as promptness, reliability, diligence, and a strong work ethic. Beyond these, there are more nuanced skills that do not have anything to do with any one specific job, but make a person well suited for a particular field. For example, many jobs in the computers and programming field are ideal for people who are detail-oriented, creative, can think logically, and enjoy solving problems. Finally, there are transferrable skills—these skills may not have anything to do with computers and programming, per se, but they can certainly help you in that line of work. For example, a person who has experience in bookkeeping might do well as a database administrator. A person who has experience in retail sales might find those skills transfer well to a computer support position. A person who has excellent math skills may find software programming enables him or her to utilize those skills on another level. Someone who has experience in marketing may find striking out on their own as an Internet entrepreneur appealing.

Define Your Ideal Job

This is more than just a title. When clarifying this in your mind, consider things like the skills you feel you are strongest in and that you want to utilize (or perhaps skills you do not yet possess but want to become proficient in—by developing those skills you can further advance your career!). Consider the work environment you would find ideal: working at home, working for a small company, working for a large company, working a traditional 40-hour-a-week job, working whatever hours a job requires, or perhaps being on call. The environment also extends to the people. Those who want to be surrounded by people who are more creative might be better suited working for a gaming or CGI company. Those who are passionate about giving back to the community may find themselves drawn to a nonprofit that specializes in providing computers for libraries and schools. Location is another factor to consider. Do you want to work in a particular city, such as Seattle, San Diego, or Singapore? Have you had enough of winters in Minnesota and decided that life in Florida is better suited for you? And then there is income. Some people want to make $100,000 a year; for others, $40,000 is sufficient. Keep in mind that you may have to start with the $40,000 salary to get to the $100,000 one.

Make the Most of Your Time

It is not how hard you search—rather, the key is how smartly you search. According to Kate Wendleton, president of the Five O'Clock Club, a national outplacement and career counseling network, 6 percent of jobs are found through listings and ads and 3 percent are found through recruiters and search firms. Combine these with the aforementioned Department of Labor statistics, and it is clear networking is the most effective job-hunting tool at your disposal. Make a list of all the people you know—both those who might be of help to you directly in your job search and those who might not (you never know who those people know). Contact these people, explain that you are looking to launch a new career, and ask them if they can recommend any possible leads. Be professional and be concise, but do not be afraid to ask. Worst-case scenario, they will not be able to help you. Best-case scenario, they lead you to your ideal job. As mentioned, contact companies you are interested in—even if they aren't currently advertising any open positions—and ask if you can send them your résumé.

And Speaking of Résumés

There is no need to spend a lot of time designing your résumé. Templates abound on the Internet, and this is really a case where simple is better and content trumps a glitzy-looking résumé with no real substance. Peter Vogt, MonsterTRAK Career Coach for Monster. com, warns job seekers to be aware of the following mistakes in résumés and provides advice on avoiding them.

A résumé must be grammatically perfect. If it is not, employers will assume that you either do not care enough about your job search to be bothered or that you cannot write or that you really do not have an eye for detail after all. Have at least one other person check your résumé before you start sending it out. Better yet, have two or three people check it.

Be specific. Employers need to understand what you have done and accomplished. For example, rather than saying, "Managed databases for a large image catalog company," say, "Managed 1,500 databases for Getty Images and supervised four other database administrators."

While the bulk of your résumé can be used throughout your job search, you must tailor your résumé so that it is specific to the job you are applying for. Clearly show how and why you fit the position in a specific organization. Highlight accomplishments instead of duties. While it might be easier to just list what you did in your day-to-day tasks, such as "Updated departmental files," employers are more concerned with what you accomplished while carrying out these day-to-day tasks. For example: "Reorganized 10 years worth of unwieldy files, making them easily accessible to department members."

In general, a résumé should be about one to two pages in length. However, there are no real rules here. Different employers have different expectations and prefer different things. Naturally, someone who is just out of college and new to the workplace will have a shorter résumé than someone who has been in the workplace for 10. Again, the most important thing is what the résumé contains, not how long it is.

As for the length of a résumé, some employers like to see an objective statement on a résumé; others do not care for them or skip over them. It does not hurt to include one, but avoid vague, meaningless statements such as "Seeking a challenging position that offers professional growth." Rather, make your objective statement specific and tailor it for the employer in question. For example: "Seeking a challenging entry-level computer support position that allows me to contribute my skills and experience in customer service to help people solve problems." Use "action" words and avoid passive writing. For example, rather than saying "Responsible for answering user questions and addressing complaints," say, "Resolved user questions as part of an IT help desk serving 4,000 users and staff."

Do not assume you know what an employer will or will not think is important when detailing your job history. For example, you might not think that working as a camp counselor during the summers to earn money for school is important, but these are skills that are both potentially transferrable and demonstrate what kind of a worker you are. Evidence of these skills is more important to employers than you might think.

Your résumé should be visually appealing. You might think your résumé looks great with four different fonts, bold, italic, and underlining; and maybe you have squeezed in text so that what originally fit on one and a half pages now fits on one. However, if your résumé is hard to read and hard on the eyes, it is likely to get passed over. Just as you should have a few people check your résumé for grammatical and typographical errors, have them look at it strictly from a visual standpoint, too, and make sure your résumé is easy on the eyes. Double-check all the details—this includes your address, phone numbers, and e-mail address. The most stellar résumé in the world does no good if the contact information is wrong.

Finally, no matter how well or how poorly you thought the interview went, it is important that you follow up immediately after the interview. Either later that day or the next day (but no later), send a handwritten thank-you note to the person who interviewed you.

It may seem like a minor detail, but one executive at a nonprofit continuing education company reported that one of things that gave a particular applicant an edge over the others was that she was the only one to send a thank-you note afterwards.

The Art of Interviewing

While you may dread the thought of being interviewed, the fact is that you are not likely to land a job without one—even if it is just a phone interview. The more practice you can gain in honing your interview skills, the better. And be prepared for the unexpected. Some companies conduct one-on-one interviews, others conduct interviews where a group of four or more people are asking questions. If someone totally unrelated to the group you are interviewing for performs the interview, take it seriously. It may well be a tiebreaker interview. The sections that follow will provide essential tips for interviewing—both what to do and what not to do.

Things That Can Make or Break Your Interview

What you wear really does matter. Even if the corporate culture at the company is casual and laid back with regard to work attire, that does not mean you should dress that way for your interview. You do not necessarily need to wear a business suit, but your clothes should be clean and wrinkle-free, with no rips or tears. Wear slacks rather than jeans.

Make eye contact when you first meet the person who greets you for your interview, once or twice again while walking to the interview location, and again when you first sit down to do the interview. Shake the person's hand firmly. Act professional and confident.

Make sure you ask questions during the interview. Granted, you are the one being interviewed, but keep in mind that you are also interviewing this company (or this department if you are moving from one group to another inside a company). Read up on the company, the business, and the business group. Investigate the company and the position as thoroughly as you can. Write down at least five questions that you can ask in the interview. If you really want to land a job, be as prepared for the interview as you can. The fact that you have questions may be what sets you apart from other candidates; not asking questions could very well be the one thing that keeps you from getting the job.

Along with thoroughly understanding everything you can about the position you are applying for, know how to position your current skills against the job you are after. For example, if your experience up to this point as a network analyst involved supporting 50 computers, you might be feeling confident and worldly—until you find out that the job you are interviewing for requires that you work with customers with 20,000 computers.

According to author and career coach Mike Farr, while it is impossible to be prepared to answer every single question an employer may ask you, if you are prepared to answer the tough ones that invariably come up, you should be able to handle most any question the interviewer throws your way. These questions are:

- ➡ Why should I hire you?
- ➡ What can you tell me about yourself?
- ➡ What are your major strengths?
- ➡ What are your major weaknesses?
- ➡ What sort of pay do you expect to receive?
- ➡ How does your previous experience relate to the jobs we have here?
- ➡ What are your plans for the future?
- ➡ What will your former employer (or references) say about you?
- ➡ Why are you looking for this type of position, and why here?

Ask friends to conduct mock interviews with you and to assess how you answer these questions. Honesty is important here. They need to tell you where they felt your answers fell flat and where you came across as confident.

Other Important Skills for Success

While the information in the following sections applies to nearly every career, not just Internet-related ones, it is worth including here. Some of these tips may be reminders of things already known; others may be new to you. Some are more applicable to people who work in a large corporate setting; others apply to even the sole proprietor. All can help you maintain a professional reputation at all times, which naturally helps your career move forward.

Effective Business Communication Techniques

One of the most important skills a person in an Internet-related career can have is the ability to talk "techspeak" to those who might not be so knowledgeable. Learn how to explain concepts in a way that is not demeaning to the nontechnical person, yet assures understanding—and do not talk down to people. Make sure the nontechies are satisfied with the explanation and all questions have been answered.

This is also important when in meetings or similar situations where, for example, a user interface designer or software developer is explaining how the content management software's technical requirements are greater than anticipated and require more resources sooner rather than later. Avoid slipping into overuse of jargon and acronyms. Just because you are familiar with these terms does not mean everyone else around you is. Also, this concept is important to keep in mind no matter what form your communication is in—whether face-to-face, on the phone, via e-mail or instant messaging, or a business proposal, keep your audience and their level of understanding about what it is you do in mind.

Managing Your Time Effectively

While sometimes a person can get in over their head because they overestimate their skills, in many cases this occurs because of improper time management. Developing techniques and strategies that help you manage your time effectively will, in turn, reduce your stress level and increase productivity.

When you have projects with hard and fast deadlines, prioritize your schedule accordingly. Block out this time in your schedule if you need to, and let coworkers and others know that you need to be undisturbed for a given amount of time—even if it is just an hour. That hour of concentrated work could be worth four hours of work with interruptions. If you need to (and if this is possible, given your work environment), consider working in a separate room.

Some people are at their sharpest in the morning; others are more effective in the afternoon. Know what your "best" time of the day is and tackle your most challenging tasks then. If you still find it hard to stay on task, try to figure out where the block lies. Are you lacking information to complete the tasks? Are you lacking motivation? Are you unclear about the goals? Positively identifying some of these problem areas will often lead to solutions, which, in turn, leads to better time management.

Best Practice

Stay in the Loop

If there is one constant when it comes to the Internet and its related areas, it is that change is constant, so stay in the loop! A common mistake for people in this field is to possess a certain naivety when it comes to a given area of technology. Do not misunderstand how much a software product, for example, will change over time. Content is in a nearly constant cycle of revision and behaviors or features that were part of the original design of a product (again, using software as an example) may no longer exist as the development process continues. Ask about the scope of your work on a regular basis, and make it a point to keep yourself apprised of any changes.

If you find yourself chronically behind in tasks and routinely missing deadlines, for the sake of your professional reputation, consider keeping a "time diary." Just as people who are struggling with their weight or their finances keep a log for a week or a month, noting where every penny goes or what they put in their mouth, so, too, can keeping a log of where and how you are spending your time show you where simple changes can help improve efficiency. For example, a 2007 survey conducted on behalf of Fuser.com found that 87 percent of U.S. Internet users spend at least seven hours a week managing their e-mail—that's practically an entire workday!

One well-known, effective time management technique is the basic "to do" list. Every evening, before you leave work, make a list of what you need to accomplish the next day. Prioritize it in terms of urgency and importance. Aim to achieve as much as possible, but always remain flexible so that you can take on unexpected tasks if necessary.

While it is natural to want to say "yes" to everything that is asked of you, if you try and juggle too many balls in the air at once, you are bound to drop a few—and your professional reputation can suffer. If you are asked to take on a task and you know that you will not be able to meet the deadline, you must communicate that up front. Be honest—avoid giving a vague answer like "I am not sure."

Consider negotiating on the timing. For example, say, "I cannot do it today, but I would be happy to do it by the end of the week." If this task is one you simply cannot turn down, work with your supervisor or other colleagues, explain the situation to them, and come up with a plan so that other deadlines are not missed. Learning to say no is not easy, but you will earn more respect by understanding and respecting your own limits—and communicating them clearly and effectively—rather than saying "yes" to everything and paying the price down the road.

Chapter 5

Talk Like a Pro

While it might send language purists into despair, the fact remains that the Internet has a language all its own, and has been the genesis for a wide variety of funny-sounding words and phrases. The following glossary explains these terms in detail, with information on key terminology, acronyms, jargon, phrases, concepts, and general business language that will help ensure that you are fluent in "netspeak."

ActiveX Microsoft-based technology designed to link desktop applications to the Web. With ActiveX, software developers can create interactive Web content for their applications. For example, Word and Excel documents can be viewed directly in Web browsers that support ActiveX.

Advanced Research Projects Agency (ARPA) Eventually renamed DARPA (Defense Advanced Research Projects Agency), this program was established in 1958 to protect the United States against "technological surprises," such as when the Soviet Union launched *Sputnik* into space in 1957, beating the United States in the "space race." This agency is responsible for the development of new technology for use by the military, and has been responsible for funding the development of many technologies, including computer networking.

adware Software that displays ads while a program is running.

AFAIK "As far as I know"

AFK "Away from keyboard"

agnostic   A term that refers to a software platform, application, or other device that will run on any operating system.

algorithmic authority   Defined by Clay Shirky, an adjunct professor of new media at New York University, as "the decision to regard as authoritative an unmanaged process of extracting value from diverse, untrustworthy sources, without any human [verification]."

alpha   A product that is in the alpha stage of development contains all of the features necessary to operate for its intended purpose and is ready for testing. Unlike beta testing, alpha testing is done entirely internally, by the publisher, developers, and other team members.

alpha geek   Jargon referring to the most knowledgeable, technically competent person in an office or workgroup.

analog   As the word pertains to computing, it refers to a computer that uses continuous electrical, mechanical, or hydraulic quantities to model the problem being solved. With an analog computer, numbers are represented by directly measurable quantities, such as voltages or rotations.

Anticybersquatting Consumer Protection Act (ACPA)   A law that gives trademark owners legal remedies against people who obtain domain names that are identical to or so similar to the trademark as to be confusing.

applet   Simple, single-function programs that often ship with a larger product. Examples include the Calculator, File Manager, and Notepad that come with Windows.

application programming interface (API)   A set of routines used by a program to direct the performance of procedures by an operating system. APIs can be language-independent (utilizing the particular syntax and elements of a programming language) or language-independent (written so that they can be called from several programming languages).

artificial intelligence   Also known simply as "AI," this field of computer science has to do with the intelligence of machines. John McCarthy, an American computer scientist, coined the term in 1956 as "the science and engineering of making intelligent machines."

assembler   A device that converts assembly language code into machine code.

assembly language   Low-level programming languages that used symbolic representations of numeric machine codes and other constants needed to program a particular CPU architecture—in other words, a human-readable form of a computer's internal language. Each type of processor has its own assembly language. Assembly languages are now used mainly for optimizing speed-sensitive parts of code.

avatar   A character in a game who represents and is controlled by the player. Prominent examples include characters in a first-person shooter game or the characters players can create in such virtual worlds as *Second Life*.

B2B   An acronym for "business to business," this term refers to commerce-based transactions between businesses, whether a manufacturer and a wholesaler or a manufacturer and a retailer.

B2C   An acronym for "business to consumer," this term refers to business selling a product or service directly to the customer.

BAK   "Back at keyboard"

bandwidth theft   Also referred to as hot linking or direct linking, this is the practice of directly linking images, scripts, movies, or other files to a Web site from another site's server without the owner's permission or knowledge, which causes that owner to incur costly charges for the extra bandwidth consumed.

BBL   "Be back later"

BD   "Big deal"

beta   A term referring to new software or hardware that either is being updated or is ready to be released to a select group of users for testing. In beta testing, potential customers and users test the functionality of the product and report any errors found. This is typically one of the last steps in development before a product is released to market.

BFN   "Bye for now"

binary   With regard to computing, this term refers to the system of representing text or program instructions through the use of a two-digit number system: 0 represents the "off" state; 1 represents the "on" state.

bit   A piece of data represented by either a zero or a one.

blog   A contraction of the term *Web log*, this is an online journal or diary. Many are maintained by an individual, and typically provide commentary on news, current events, or a particular topic.

blogosphere   The collective community of bloggers and the network of interconnected blogs. The phrase came about because so many blogs link to one another.

Fast Facts

Top Sites

Alexa.com, a Web information company, regularly looks at Web site traffic in a given month. By combining the average daily visitors with the number of page views, the highest-ranking sites on the Internet can be obtained. As of January 3, 2010, the top 20 sites on the Web were:

- Google (http://www.google.com)
- Facebook (http://www.facebook.com)
- YouTube (http://www.youtube.com)
- Yahoo! (http://www.yahoo.com)
- Windows Live (http://www.live.com)
- Wikipedia (http://www.wikipedia.org)
- Blogger.com (http://www.blogger.com)
- Baidu.com (http://www.baidu.com)
- Microsoft Network (MSN) (http://www.msn.com)
- Yahoo! (Japan) (http://www.yahoo.co.jp)
- QQ.COM (http://www.qq.com – This is the site for Tencent, China's largest and most used Internet service portal)
- Google India (http://www.google.co.in)
- Twitter (http://www.twitter.com)
- MySpace (http://www.myspace.com)
- Google China (http://www.google.cn)
- SINA (http://www.sina.com.cn – a leading online media company and mobile value-added service provider in China)
- Google Germany (http://www.google.de)
- Amazon.com (http://www.amazon.com)
- WordPress.com (http://www.wordpress.com)
- Microsoft Corporation (http://www.microsoft.com)

bookmark   A pointer (often to a URL) in an Internet Web browser; a marker of one's place in an electronic document.

BRB   "Be right back"

broadband   A type of communications system in which the medium used for transmission carries multiple messages simultaneously. This form of communication is typically for wide area networks.

browse   To explore different Web sites on the Internet, clicking pages and links to see where they go. This is different from searching in that the user may not be looking for anything specific.

BTW   "By the way"

bug   An error in computer coding or logic that causes a program to function incorrectly or to produce incorrect or unexpected results.

build   The compilation of source code files into executable code. A build is not the complete software product. Rather, the build is a compilation of the files needed to operate the software with the features implemented to date. Builds are typically used during the testing process.

burn rate   A term that refers to the rate at which a company will use up (burn) its shareholder capital, thus incurring a negative cash flow. The term came into common use during the dot-com era, when many start-up companies went through several stages of funding before ultimately becoming profitable or going bankrupt and closing down.

byte   A byte is made up of eight bits. These groups of eight bits can represent up to 256 different values and can correspond to a variety of different symbols, letters, or instructions.

cache   A temporary storage area where frequently accessed data can be stored for rapid access. Once data is stored in the cache, it can be accessed from here rather than being retrieved or calculated again. This cuts down on access time.

central processing unit (CPU)   A single chip, such as a microprocessor, or a series of chips that performs arithmetic and logical calculations, and that times and controls the operations of the other elements of the system.

chat room   An Internet site where several users can have online conversations in real time. These chats can involve as few as two people or as many as the bandwidth allows. Most chat rooms are devoted to a specific topic, but some are more general.

chip jewelry   Jargon for old, outdated computers destined for the junk pile or turned into decorative ornaments.

click-through rate (CTR)   A common way to measure the success of an online advertising campaign, obtained by dividing the number of users who clicked on an ad by the number of times the page was delivered.

client   Software that accesses a remote service on another computer.

cloud computing   A style of computing in which real-time scalable resources are provided "as a service over the Internet to users who need not have knowledge of, expertise in, or control over the technology infrastructure that supports them," according to authors Galen Gruman and Eric Knorr. The term "cloud" is a metaphor for the Internet, based on how it is depicted in computer network diagrams, and is an abstraction for the complex infrastructure it conceals.

cobweb site   A Web site that has not been updated for a long time or is inactive.

compiler   A computer program that transforms source code written in one computer language (called the source language) into another computer language (called the target language).

concern   A particular set of behaviors needed by a computer program. A concern can be as general as database interaction or as specific as performing a calculation.

cookie   A simple piece of data that a Web server stores on a client system. It is used to identify users, to instruct the server to send a customized version of a particular Web page, to submit account information, and so on.

cookie poisoning   Modifying a cookie in order to gain unauthorized permission about a user for nefarious purposes, such as identity theft.

cross-cutting concern   Aspects of a program that affect other concerns. These concerns often cannot be easily broken down from the rest of the system in either design or implementation, and result in scattering or tangling of the program or both.

cyberslacking   A term that refers to using one's Internet access at work to accomplish personal tasks while appearing to be carrying out one's work duties.

cyberstalking   Using information and communications technology, particularly the Internet, to harass another person. This behavior can include false accusations, monitoring, the transmission of threats, identity theft, damage to data or equipment, the solicitation of minors for sexual purposes, and gathering information for harassment purposes.

daemon Pronounced "demon," this Unix-related term refers to a specific type of program or agent designed to work in the background while other programs are running carrying out more important tasks.

data compression Also known as source coding, this is the process of encoding information using fewer bits than an unencoded representation would use through use of specific encoding schemes. Data compression is typically carried out by algorithms that find and remove redundancies in data.

data mining The process of identifying commercially useful patterns or relationships in large amounts of data. While the term has acquired a somewhat negative connotation in recent years, at its heart, it is simply the process of turning raw data into useful information. It is what enables sites like Netflix to recommend other movies you might enjoy based on your (and others') recent picks.

dead tree edition Jargon for the paper version of a publication that is available in both print and electronic forms.

debugger A programming tool that allows a programmer to monitor and modify a program as it runs.

deep-linking A hyperlink that bypasses a Web site's home page and takes a user directly to an internal page.

desktop Characteristic of programs such as Microsoft Windows and Apple Macintosh, this term refers to the on-screen work area that uses icons and menus in such a way that it simulates how a person uses a physical desktop to manage tasks and workflow.

digital This term refers to a computer system that uses discrete (discontinuous) values, usually but not always symbolized numerically, to represent information for input, processing, transmission, storage, etc. By contrast, analog systems use a continuous range of values to represent information. Although digital representations are discrete, the information represented can be either discrete (numbers, letters, or icons) or continuous (sounds or images).

digital certificate A password-protected file that includes a variety of information, such as the name and e-mail address of the certificate holder, an encryption key that can be used to verify the digital signature of the holder, the name of the company issuing the certificate, and the period during which the certificate is valid.

Digital Subscriber Line (DSL)   A high-speed Internet service that operates over standard copper telephone lines, like dial-up service, but is many times faster than dial-up. In addition, DSL does not tie up the phone line. Thus, users can surf the Internet and use the phone at the same time.

domain name   An identifying label that defines a realm of administrative autonomy, authority, or control in the Internet, based on the domain name system (DNS).

domain name registry   A database of all domain names registered in a top-level domain.

dot-com   A term referring to a company that does most, if not all, of its business on the Internet. Common usage, however, generally refers to the business boom and bust that came into being in the late 1990s and ended in early 2000.

download   To transfer information from a remote computer to the computer a person is working on.

drive-by download   A jargon term that refers to a program that is automatically and invisibly downloaded to a user's computer, often without the user's knowledge or consent.

driver   A hardware device or program that controls or regulates another device. The term is commonly used in conjunction with devices such as printers or disk drives. A print driver, for example, enables a computer and printer to communicate and work together.

e-commerce   Short for "electronic commerce," this refers to the buying and selling of products and services over the Internet.

egosurfing   Jargon for surfing the Internet looking for mention of your name; also becoming known as "Googling yourself."

electronic data interchange (EDI)   Going beyond e-mail, this term refers to the structured transmission of data between organizations by electronic means. It is used primarily to transfer electronic documents from one computer system to another. The term also refers to a specific set of standards.

electronic funds transfer (EFT)   A computer-based system used to perform financial transactions electronically. This can refer to a wide range to transactions, from online payments to a transfer between bank accounts to balance inquiries.

e-mail   Short for electronic mail, at its heart, this is an electronic text message, but can include the transmission of files, applications, graphics, and more.

e-mail spoofing   Forging an e-mail header so that the message appears to have come from the original source legitimately.

emoticon   Text-based faces and objects often used in e-mail and online chat. They help give the reader a sense of the writer's feelings behind the text. Emoticons can also be used to create objects, such as a flower. Perhaps the most common emoticon is :) which represents a smiley face.

encryption   The process of transforming data into a form that can be read only by the intended receiver. To decipher the message, the receiver of the encrypted data must have the proper decryption key.

engine   An aspect of a computer program that performs a particular task, often on an ongoing basis.

Ethernet   A standard by which local area networks are connected by coaxial cable, fiber-optic cable, or twisted-pair wiring in a bus or star topology.

executable file   The end product of the programming process. This is the file that is ready to be run on a computer.

extranet   An extension of a company's intranet using World Wide Web technology. An extranet is often used to allow a company's customers, suppliers, and others to gain limited access to the company's intranet for specific purposes.

fair use   While this term is more commonly understood as applying to copyright law, it can also be applied to broadband capacity. Under the Fair Access Policy, a bandwidth cap (also known as a bit cap) limits the transfer of a specified amount of data over a given period. Internet service providers commonly apply a cap when a channel intended to be shared by many users becomes overloaded, or may be overloaded, by a few users.

fiber optics   A technology that uses light beams to transmit information along optical fibers. Light has a higher frequency than other types of radiation, such as radio waves, and a single fiber-optic channel can carry more information that most other forms of transmission. As of this writing, some companies are starting to offer Internet and television service over fiber-optic lines.

File Transfer Protocol (FTP)   The protocol used for copying files to and from remote computer systems on a network.

filter   Software programs that can block access to designated Web sites that contain inappropriate or potentially offensive material by scanning for certain words and phrases.

firewall   A device that is either hardware or software based that limits the data that can pass through it and protects a networked server or client machine from damage by unauthorized users.

firmware   Permanent commands, data, or programs that the computer needs to function correctly.

framing   Allowing a user to view a second Web site "framed" in the information of the first Web site.

freeware   Software that can be downloaded and distribute for free. The software is still protected by a copyright, however, so a person cannot pass it off as his or her own creation.

function   Also known as a subroutine, this is the purpose of or action carried out by a program or routine.

functional programming   A style of programming in which the evaluation of expressions is emphasized rather than the carrying out of commands. Examples include APL, Lisp, Kite, and Opal.

future-proof   Jargon for a term that supposedly will not become outdated anytime soon.

FWIW   "For what it's worth"

gigabyte   A unit of information equal to 1,000 megabytes.

GMTA   "Great minds think alike"

graphical user interface   A type of operating environment that represents programs, files, and options through the use of menus, icons, and dialog boxes. A user selects and activates these items by pointing and clicking with a mouse or using a keyboard.

"green" computing   The study and practice of using computing resources efficiently. The goals are to reduce the use of hazardous materials, maximize energy efficiency during the product's lifetime, and promote recyclability or biodegradability of defunct products and factory waste.

hack   While the term often has nefarious connotations, it simply refers to creatively altering the behavior or an application or operating system by modifying its code rather than running the program and using it in the traditional manner.

hard disk   This is a storage device on which data can be recorded magnetically. This is often used interchangeably with the term "hard drive." However, these are not the same things. The hard drive is what houses the hard disk and reads and writes data to it.

hardware The physical components of a computer system, such as printers, mice, keyboards, and the case.

host A computer that provides Web documents to clients or users. This is the same thing as a Web server.

hotlinking Also known as inline linking, leeching, piggy-backing, direct linking, offsite image grabs and bandwidth theft, hotlinking is the use of a linked object, often an image, from one site into a Web page belonging to a second site.

HTH "Hope this helps"

hypertext Coined in 1965 by Ted Nelson, an American sociologist, philosopher, and pioneer of information technology, the term refers to text with references (called hyperlinks) to other text that the reader can immediately follow, usually by a mouse click. The World Wide Web is the largest example of hypertext.

Hypertext Markup Language (HTML) The standard language used for Web pages. Special identifiers, called tags, are used to indicate paragraph breaks, line spacing, font type, font size, graphics, and more. HTML indicates to the Web browser how a Web page should be displayed.

Hypertext Transfer Protocol (HTTP) The client/server protocol used to access information on the World Wide Web.

IAE "In any event"

identity theft Obtaining key pieces of personal information, such as a Social Security number or driver's license number, in order to impersonate another person and gain monetarily or in some other fashion.

IMHO "In my humble opinion"

IMNSHO "In my not so humble opinion"

instance In object-oriented programming, this is an object in relation to the class in which it belongs. An instance may contain data or instructions.

instant messaging (IM) A form of real-time text-based communication between two or more people using shared clients. The text is conveyed via devices connected over a network such as the Internet.

integrated development environment (IDE) An application that combines an editor, compiler, linker, debugger, and so on into a single tool so that work can be carried out in one application instead of switching back and forth between several.

intellectual property   A general term referring to copyrights, patents, trademarks, and trade secrets.

Internet Corporation for Assigned Names and Numbers (ICANN)   The organization responsible for overseeing the registration of domain names.

Internet service provider   A company that provides access to the Internet.

intranet   A network designed for use within a company or organization. It often uses applications associated with the Internet, such as Web pages, FTP sites, and e-mail, but is accessible only to those within the company or organization.

IOW   "In other words"

IP telephony   Also called Voice over Internet Protocol (VoIP), this term refers to a family of transmission technologies for the delivery of voice communications over IP networks such as the Internet or other packet-switched networks.

IQueue   Jargon for the line of interesting or noteworthy e-mail messages to be read after the junk mail has been deleted.

IYSWIM   "If you see what I mean"

Java   A software platform technology developed by Sun Microsystems, Inc., that provides a means of developing application software and deploying it in a cross-platform environment. Java is used in a wide variety of computing platforms, from embedded devices and mobile phones, to enterprise servers and supercomputers.

J/K   "Just kidding"

kernel   The core of an operating system. It manages memory, files, and peripheral devices; maintains the time and date; launches applications; and allocates system resources.

keyboard shortcut   A combination of keystrokes that performs a certain command, such as closing a window or saving a file. For example, pressing CTRL-S in Windows can save a document that is being worked on. On a Mac, the keyboard shortcut to paste copied data is COMMAND-V.

keyword search advertising   Sponsored areas of search engine result listings, such as Google's AdWords, where certain ads appear based on relevant keywords.

killer app   Any computer program that is so necessary or desirable that it proves the core value of some larger technology, such as a gaming console, operating system, or other software.

A killer app can substantially increase sales of the platform on which it runs. For example, the *Halo* series of video games produced for Xbox is considered a killer app.

kilobyte A unit of data consisting of 1,024 bytes. Often abbreviated as K, KB, or Kbyte.

language A specific pattern of binary digital information.

laptop A small, portable computer that, these days, is nearly as powerful as its desktop brethren. Most can run the same software as a desktop computer and can use similar peripheral devices, such as mice, sound cards, and external drives.

lifecycle The stages a software product goes through, from the initial concept, to development, to testing, to release.

linker A tool that binds different modules of a program together into a single executable file.

listserv E-mailed compilations of newsgroup or forum postings.

local area network (LAN) A group of computers and other devices dispersed over a relatively small area and connected by a link that enables devices and computers to communicate with one another.

logic programming A type of programming in which a program consists of facts and relationships, from which the language is expected to draw conclusions based on these facts.

LOL "Laugh out loud"

loop A set of statements in a program that is executed repeatedly either a fixed number of times or until a condition is true or false.

lossless compression A data-compression technique that preserves all data, enabling it to be decompressed back into a file identical to the original.

lossy compression A data-compression technique that results in some information being irretrievably lost. Lossy compression may be used when this loss of information is not significant—for example, in video or audio, where the missing data is not likely to be noticed.

LTNS "Long time no see"

machine Jargon often used to refer to a computer—that is, the physical machine.

machine code A system of instructions and data executed directly by a computer's central processing unit.

macro A set of keystrokes and related instructions that are recorded and saved under a short key code or macro name.

When the set of keystrokes is typed or pressed, the instructions are carried out.

mail bomb Sending a massive amount of e-mail to a specific person or network with the intention of disrupting service or denying access.

mainframe Also called a "supercomputer," this is a high-level computer designed for intensive computing tasks. A mainframe computer is often shared by multiple users, who connect to it through terminals.

malware An umbrella term combining the words malicious and software, and used to refer to a variety of forms of hostile, intrusive, or annoying software or program code, such as worms, viruses, Trojan horses, and more.

memory A device where information can be stored and retrieved. This may be a tape drive or a disk drive (external devices), or the RAM that is connected directly to the computer.

message board A Web page where users post and reply to messages. These messages remain on the page indefinitely and are even archived in some cases for later access.

meta-tags Relevant key words used by search engines to index pages, allowing Web users to find tagged pages in searches.

method In object-oriented programming, this is a process performed by an object when it receives a message.

microprocessor Also called the central processing unit (CPU), this is the device that interprets and carries out instructions—in other words, it is the "brain" of the computer.

middleware Computer software that connects other software components or applications. It includes Web servers, application servers, and similar tools that support application development and delivery.

motherboard The main circuit board of a computer, containing the primary components of the system: the processor, main memory, bus controller, connector, and support circuitry.

mouse-trapping Jargon referring to a Web site that a visitor cannot leave without clicking on a succession of pop-up windows.

multimedia The combination of sound, graphics, and video. This can also refer to a subset of hypermedia, which combines these elements with hypertext.

multiprocessing The use of two or more central processing units within a single computer system. Also, to the ability of a system to support more than one processor and/or the ability to allocate tasks between them. The objective in any case is increased speed and computing power.

multitasking The ability of a computer system to work on more than one task at a time.

natural language Any language that is spoken, signed, or written by humans for general-purpose communication. Compare to computer language, which is a machine-readable artificial language designed to express computations that can be performed by a machine, namely, a computer.

netbook A small, portable computer that relies on wireless communication for access to the Internet. Netbooks are designed primarily for sending and receiving e-mail and browsing the Web. With not much more in the way of capabilities, it can be thought of as a slimmed-down laptop.

netiquette A term that refers to polite behavior and good manners on the Internet. It basically involves respecting others' privacy and doing one's best not to deliberately annoy other people. Three areas where good netiquette is highly stressed are e-mail, online chat, and newsgroups.

Netscape This term refers to both a browser and the name of a company. The browser once dominated the market share and was based on the Mosaic program developed at the National Center for Supercomputing Applications, but lost this edge to Internet Explorer. By the end of 2006, the usage share of Netscape browsers had fallen, from over 90 percent in the mid-1990s, to less than 1 percent.

netspeak A type of slang that Internet users have popularized, and in many cases, have coined. Such terms often originate with the purpose of saving keystrokes (consider LOL for "laughing out loud"). Acronyms, keyboard symbols and shortened words are often used as methods of abbreviation in Internet slang.

network A group of computers and associated devices that are connected either permanently (through cables, for example) or temporarily (such as through a telephone connection). Networks can range in size from just a few users to a large geographic area.

neural network With regard to computer science (bioinformatics, in particular), this term refers to a network of interconnected programming constructs that imitate the properties of biological neurons (called artificial neurons). These are often used to gain an understanding of biological neural networks or to solve artificial intelligence problems.

node   As it relates to networking, a node is a device that facilitates communication with other network devices. A router or even a computer can act as a node. As it relates to data structures, a node is a location that stores data and links to one or more nodes below it—think of it as a building block of sorts.

notwork   Jargon for a network in a nonworking state.

Keeping in Touch

Twitter Tips

The social networking site Twitter can be used for more than just letting friends and family know what you are up to. It can also be a valuable business tool. Business and companies use Twitter to keep their customers up-to-date on products, services, and special offers; to gather real-time feedback on their performance; and to build business relationships, among other things. So how can Twitter help your Internet-based career? The Twitter Web site offers the following tips:

- Include in your bio and/or custom background the names of the people twittering from your company account. Include additional contact info, as well, like e-mail addresses.

- Listen regularly for comments about your company, brand, and products—and be prepared to address concerns, offer customer service, or thank people for praise.

- While you should not feel compelled to follow everyone who follows you, do respond to some questions or comments addressed to you.

- Post links to articles and sites you think folks would find interesting—even if they are not your sites or about your company.

- Make sure your tweets provide some real value. For example, offer Twitter-exclusive coupons or deals, take people behind the scenes of your company, or post pictures from your offices, stores, etc.

NP "No problem"

NRN "No reply necessary"

NW "No way"

object file The output of a compiler or assembler, this file contains machine code, but cannot be run by a computer until it is linked to other object files and forms an executable file.

object-oriented programming In terms of software, a program is viewed as a collection of discrete objects that are themselves collections of self-contained collections of data structures that interact with other objects.

open access A term that applies to free-to-use learning objects and resources—that is, materials that do not require a license for use. Most open-access material is distributed via the World Wide Web, but is free to redistribute online as well as offline.

open content Copyrighted information that is made available by the copyright owner to the general public under license terms that allow reuse of the material, often with the requirement that the person reusing the material grant these same rights to the modified version.

open source In reference to computer programming, this term refers to the free exchange and collaboration of developers and producers. The definition put forth by Bruce Perens, a well-known computer programmer, is widely recognized as the "real" definition: "A broad, general type of software license that makes source code available to the general public with relaxed or nonexistent copyright restrictions."

operator A symbol or other character indicating an operation that acts on one or more elements.

OTOH "On the other hand"

packet A unit of information that is transmitted in its entirety from one device to another on a network.

packet switching A message-delivery technique in which small units of information (packets) are relayed through stations in a computer network along the best route available between the source and the destination. The Internet is an example of a packet-switching network.

password A code used to gain access to a locked system, whether this be a network or a single computer. Strong passwords contain letter and non-letter characters, are not simple combinations, and are not easily guessed.

patch   Downloadable software that fixes bugs or adds features to a product after it has already shipped.

peer to peer (P2P)   Any distributed network architecture composed of participants that make a portion of their resources (such as processing power, disk storage or network bandwidth) directly available to other network participants, without the need for central coordination instances (such as servers or hosts). Peers are both suppliers and consumers of resources. P2P was popularized by file-sharing systems like Napster.

peripheral device   An ancillary device connected to a computer and controlled by it. Examples include (but are not limited to) speakers, joysticks, keyboards, mice, modems, and printers.

permalink   Jargon for a permanent link to a particular posting in a blog. A permalink points to a specific blog posting, however, rather than to the page in which the original posting occurred.

pharming   Redirecting a Web site's traffic to another, bogus Web site. Pharming can be conducted either by changing the host's file on a victim's computer or by exploiting a vulnerability in DNS server software.

phishing   This is an e-mail attempt by someone to gain personal information for nefarious uses. Phishing e-mails may appear to be from a legitimate source, such as a bank, and often trick the recipient to verify personal information, like an account number or Social Security number, by claiming that an account is in danger of being closed, for example. The recipient, believing the e-mail is genuine, provides the desired information, opening him- or herself up to potential identity theft.

PHP   A programming language used to create software that is part of a Web site. It is read and processed by the Web server, in contrast to HTML, which is read and processed by the Web browser.

ping   To check that a server is still running. The name comes from the sound commonly attributed to sonar systems.

pixel   The smallest unit of information in an image.

platform   As it pertains to computers, this term refers to a hardware architecture or software framework (including application frameworks) that allows software to run. Typical platforms include a computer's architecture, operating system, programming languages, and related runtime libraries or graphical user interface.

Plug and Play   A capability developed by Microsoft for its Windows 95 and later operating systems that gives users the ability to plug a device into a computer and have the computer recognize automatically that the device is there and install it.

plug-in   A small piece of software that adds features to a larger piece of software.

pod burping   Jargon for using a portable media device to insert viruses or malicious code into a corporate network.

podcast   A series of digital media files, usually audio or video, that is made available for download via Web syndication. The syndication aspect is what separates podcasts from other files accessible by direct download or streaming.

pod slurping   Jargon for using an iPod or other high-end MP3 player device as a portable hard drive in order to steal corporate files.

point of service (POS)   A device by which sales transactions can be directly debited to a customer's bank account.

Point to Point Protocol (PPP)   The most common protocol used to connect home computers to the Internet over regular phone lines.

port   This term typically refers to the place where information goes into and comes out of a computer. For example, a serial port can be used to connect a modem.

portable document format (PDF)   A file format designed to enable the viewing and printing of documents with all their formatting intact, regardless of what operating system is used. Developed by the Adobe Corporation, the PDF format is based on the Postscript document description language.

Portable Network Graphics (PNG)   A graphics format specifically designed for use on the Web. It enables the compression of images without a loss in quality.

portal   A Web site that functions as a point of access to any kind of information on the Internet.

posting   A message entered in a network communications systems, whether it is a message board, a social networking site, or a blog.

processor   Also called the central processing unit (CPU), this is the device that interprets and carries out instructions—in other words, it is the "brain" of the computer.

profiler   Also called a performance analyzer, this tool helps identify where a program is spending its time so that slow routines can be identified and resolved.

program   A sequence of instructions that tells the hardware of a computer what operations to perform on data.

protocol   With regard to the Internet, this term refers to a set of "rules" that define a specific format for communication between systems. Examples include TCP, IP, HTTP, and IMAP.

proxy server   A server that acts as a go-between between a client and the server that the client is actually trying to use.

"pull" technology   A form of Internet-based communication in which data or a program is retrieved from a server to a client at the client's request. For example, using a Web browser to request a particular Web site is a form of pull technology.

"push" technology   A form of Internet-based communication in which data or a program is sent from a server to a client at the server's request. Instant messaging and e-mail are forms of push technology.

Really Simple Syndication (RSS)   A family of web feed formats used to publish and distribute frequently updated works—such as blog entries, news headlines, audio, and video—in a standardized format.

résumé   A document outlining a person's job history, duties, responsibilities, publications, and other achievements.

ROTFL/ROFL   "Rolling on the floor laughing"

router   A specially designed computer or software package that handles a connection between two or more packet-switched networks.

routine   Any section of code that can be executed within a program.

script   A type of programming language that can be used to fetch and display Web pages. Scripts can be used to build all or just part of a Web page, and can communicate with searchable databases.

search engine   A Web-based system for searching the information available on the Web.

search engine optimization (SEO)   An Internet marketing strategy that considers how users search and what they search for. For example, a Web site administrator and designer might look to improve the volume and quality of traffic to her company's Web site from search engines by including phrases in the text on Web pages that the target audience will use.

Secure Sockets Layer   A standard security technology used to establish an encrypted link between a Web server and a Web browser. It has largely been replaced by TLS.

security certificate   A piece of information, typically stored as a text file, used by the SSL protocol to establish a secure connection to a Web site.

server   A computer or software package that provides a specific kind of service to client software running on other computers. This term can refer to a certain type of server, such as a Web server, or the machine on which the software is running, such as a mail server.

servlet   A small computer program designed to add capabilities to a large piece of server software.

shareware   Software that users can try for free for a limited period, after which users are expected to register the program and pay for it. This is designed to work on the honor system, but to ensure compliance, some programs are partially disabled, stop working after a given period, or contain screens that pop up frequently to encourage users to register it.

social computing   An area of computer science concerned with where social behavior and computational systems meet. Examples include blogs, e-mail, instant messaging, social network services, wikis, and social bookmarking, as well as other kinds of software applications where people interact socially. This term has become more popular with the advent of Web 2.0.

social networking   A service that focuses on enabling virtual communities that reflect social networks or social relationships among people. Examples include Facebook and LinkedIn. One of the earliest examples was ARPANET.

software   These are the computer programs or instructions that make hardware work. In general, software can be thought of as one of two types. System software refers to a computer's operating system. Applications perform the tasks for which people use computers—for example, word processing programs, spreadsheet programs, and databases.

Software as a Service (SaaS)   A means of providing applications to customers on demand. With this type of technology, software vendors may make the application available for download on their Web site, or the application may be sent to a user's computer, laptop, cellular phone, or other device.

SOL   "Sooner or later"

spam   Unsolicited e-mail, generally sent to many users at once.

spider   Also known as a crawler, knowledge-bot, or knowbot, this is a computer program used by search engines to roam the

World Wide Web, visit sites and databases, and keep the search engine database of Web pages up-to-date. They obtain new pages, update known pages, and delete obsolete ones. Their findings are then integrated into the "home" database.

spyware   Computer software that is installed surreptitiously on a personal computer to intercept or take partial control over the user's interaction with the computer, without his or her specific consent. Spyware programs can collect various types of personal

Best
Practice

Using Facebook

More than just a way to keep in touch with friends and family, Facebook can also help you market your online business. In fact, according to a case study on Facebook, in a 12-month period, CM Photographics, a wedding photography company in Minnesota, generated nearly $40,000 in revenue directly from a $600 advertising investment on Facebook. Of the Facebook users who were directed to CM Photographics' Web site from the ads, "60 percent became qualified leads and actively expressed interest in more information." So how can you make Facebook work for you? Keep the following tips in mind:

- **Update your Facebook page often:** While the page does not need to be updated hourly—or even daily—it should be updated at least once a week, two or three times if you can manage it. By updating your page regularly, you encourage visitors to return to your site. And do not post mundane items like what you are wearing to a meeting or what you had for breakfast. Make sure any information you post, including links, photos, and updates, are relevant to your business.

- **Speaking of photos . . . :** Make sure your page has them! Photos add interest and help set your Facebook page apart from your competition. As with updates, make sure the photos are relevant to your business and help promote it.

- **Use the discussion boards and blog tools:** Both of these items can provide a way for you to communicate with customers and clients directly, soliciting feedback and get ideas.

information, such as Internet surfing habits and sites that have been visited, and can also interfere with user control of the computer in other ways, such as installing additional software and redirecting Web browser activity.

stop words   Small, frequently occurring words, such as *and*, *or*, *in*, *of*, and *the*, that are often ignored when used as search terms because they are so common as to be practically irrelevant for search purposes.

Structured Query Language (SQL)   A language used to send queries to databases. Its scope includes data query and update, schema creation and modification, and data access control.

subroutine   Another word for routine; however, it usually refers to sections of code that are short and called on a more frequent basis.

Symmetric Digital Subscriber Line (SDSL)   A type of DSL in which upload and download speeds are the same (this is not the case with regular DSL).

system   At its most basic level, any grouping of components that work together to perform a task are functioning as a system. A hardware system, for example, consists of the microprocessor, computer chips, circuitry, peripheral devices, and input and output devices. An operating system consists of program files, data files, and other applications used to process information.

tag   When used in relation to the Internet, this term can be used as a noun or a verb. As a noun, it refers to the basic element of HTML, XML, and similar languages, which are used to create Web pages. As a verb, it means to assign a relevant keyword (or keywords) to content ranging from blog posts to photos on Web sites.

telecommunications   The transmission and reception of data, television, sounds, faxes—any form of information—through the use of electrical or fiber-optic signals sent over wires or fibers, respectively, or through the air.

Telnet   A protocol that allows an Internet user to log on to and enter commands on a remote computer linked to the Internet.

terabyte   One thousand gigabytes.

terminal   A device used to send commands to a computer remotely.

terminal server   A specially designed computer that contains places to plug in several modems on one side and a connection to a LAN or host server on the other.

terms of service (TOS)   Rules that a person must agree to and abide by when using a Web site. Terms of service can cover a range of issues, including acceptable user behavior online, a company's marketing policies, and copyright notices.

text editor   Typically used for editing program code, this device often contains built-in features to help prevent a programmer from introducing syntax errors into the code.

time sharing   The use of a computer system by more than one user at the same time. This is achieved through multitasking—computing resources are shared so that the computer can work on more than one task at a time.

Transmission Control Protocol/Internet Protocol (TCP/IP)   A protocol developed by the Department of Defense for communication between computers. It is the de facto standard for data transmission over networks, including the Internet.

Transport Layer Security (TLS)   A protocol used to provide security over the Internet for communication purposes. It works by encrypting segments of network connections and is used in a wide range of applications, including Web browsing, e-mail, Internet faxing, instant messaging, and VoIP.

triple-dub   A slang way to refer to the "www" in a Web site address.

Trojan horse   A destructive program disguised as a game, utility, or application that seems harmless. When run, a Trojan horse does something harmful to the computer system while appearing to do something useful. The name comes from the ploy the Greeks used to finally enter the city of Troy during the Trojan War.

TTFN   "Ta-ta for now"

TTYL   "Talk to you later"

typosquatter   Jargon for someone who registers one or more Internet domain names based on the most common typos a person might make when entering a company's registered domain name, such as "goggle" instead of "google."

Uniform Resource Locator (URL)   The global address of documents and other resource on the World Wide Web. Every URL consists of the following: the scheme name (also called the protocol) followed by a colon (:); then, depending on the scheme, a host name (or an IP address), a port number, and the path name of the file to be retrieved or the program to be run; then (for programs such as CGI scripts) a query string.

Unix   A powerful, multiuser, multitasking operating system widely used in servers and workstations. It was originally developed by Ken Thompson and Dennis Ritchie at AT&T Bell Laboratories in 1969 for use on microcomputers.

upload   To transfer data from a computer being used to another computer.

Usenet   A worldwide system of discussion groups, with comments passed among hundreds of thousands of machines. Not all Usenet machines are on the Internet.

videocast   Short for "video podcast" and sometimes shortened to vidcast or vodcast, this refers to the online delivery of video on demand, similar to a podcast.

virtual private network   Network in which some of the parts are connected using the Internet, but data sent across the Internet is encrypted; thus, entire network is "virtually" private.

virus   An often-malicious program that infects a computer system by inserting copies of itself into certain files. A true computer virus can only spread from one computer to another (in some form of executable code) when its host is taken to the target computer; for instance, because a user sent it over a network or the Internet, or carried it on a removable medium such as a floppy disk, CD, or USB drive.

Voice over Internet Protocol (VoIP)   A group of technologies used to deliver voice communications over IP networks such as the Internet or other packet-switched networks. Also known as IP telephony, Internet telephony, voice over broadband (VoBB), broadband telephony, and broadband phone.

wardriving   Jargon for driving around in a vehicle with a Wi-Fi-enabled laptop, scanning for vulnerable signals in order to obtain Internet access.

Web browser   Application that uses HTML to enable a user to browse the World Wide Web (although also used to display content on internal networks and private file systems). With a browser, a user can view and interact with text, images, videos, music, games, and other information typically on a Web site.

Webinar   A conference in which live meetings or presentations can be conducted over the Internet.

Web site   The entire collection of Web pages and other information (including sound, images, and video files) that are made available through what appears to be a single location. In general, all the pages in a Web site share the same basic URL.

WHOIS   A database of domain names maintained by domain name engineers.

wide area network (WAN)   A communications network that connects geographically separated areas.

Wi-Fi   A registered trademark of the Wi-Fi Alliance (a global, nonprofit organization devoted to promoting the growth of wireless local area networks, or WLANs). A Wi-Fi device meets certain standards that promote interoperability among wireless devices, ranging from personal computers, laptops, and peripherals to smartphones.

wiki   A Web site that allows the quick and easy creation and editing of interlinked Web pages through the use of a Web browser that employs a simple markup language or text editor. Wikipedia is perhaps the best-known example.

World Wide Web   Often referred to as just "the Web" or "WWW," this is the entire collection of resources available through Web servers that connect to Web browsers to Web pages.

World Wide Web Consortium (WC3)   The mission of World Wide Web Consortium is "to lead the World Wide Web to its full potential by developing protocols and guidelines that ensure long-term growth for the Web." The organization does this by publishing open (non-proprietary) standards for Web languages and protocols.

worm   A program that propagates itself across computers, typically by creating copies of itself in each computer's memory. Unlike viruses, a worm does not need human help to spread to other computers.

WTG   "Way to go"

YMMV   "Your mileage may vary"

Chapter 6

Resources

Although this book is designed to be as comprehensive a guide as possible for those venturing forth on an Internet-based career, as the previous chapters have shown, those careers can vary widely. Many subjects in the last five chapters were touched on only briefly because an in-depth look is beyond the scope of this book. This chapter will fill in those gaps by providing additional sources of information, from relevant Web sites, to books and periodicals, and more. Use the resources listed here to get additional training or otherwise manage and advance your career.

Associations and Organizations

There is a wide range of groups and associations that are focused on various aspects of the Internet. Some are designed for Web masters, others focus on programmers and developers, still others cater to online writers and editors—there are about as many organizations as there are jobs in the Internet field. Belonging to one of these can reap all sorts of benefits, including networking and job opportunities, additional sources of knowledge, and maybe even a whole new group of friends.

Alliance of Technology and Women is a nonprofit organization that "supports women and men worldwide who share the common interests of empowering women in technology, increasing the number of women in executive roles, and encouraging women and girls to enter technology fields." (http://www.atwinternational .org)

American Home Business Association is an important site for those considering an Internet-based business, which is often a home-based business. This organization can help you decide if such a move is right for you, what business may be the best, how to negotiate various laws and regulations, and more. (http://www.homebusinessworks.com)

American Society for Information Science and Technology is aimed at information professionals "leading the search for new and better theories, techniques, and technologies to improve access to information." The group's more than 4,000 members work in a variety of industries, ranging from computer science, linguistics, management, librarianship, engineering, law, medicine, chemistry, and education. (http://asis.org/about.html)

Association for Computing and Machinery touts itself as "the premier membership organization for computing professionals, delivering resources that advance computing as a science and a profession; enable professional development; and promote policies and research that benefit society." Visitors may find the Career and Job Center particularly useful. (http://www.acm.org)

Association for Multimedia Communications "promotes understanding of technology, e-learning, and e-business." Part of the organization's mission is to help members achieve success in their chosen field. They do this by offering education and networking opportunities. Members also can search for job opportunities. (http://www.amcomm.org)

Association of Information Technology Professionals offers "opportunities for IT leadership and education through partnerships with industry, government and academia." With more than 7,000 members, the organization provides education, information on relevant IT issues, and networking forums. (http://aitp.org)

Certified Internet Web Professional Program claims to be "the world's fastest growing vendor-neutral Internet certification for the knowledge economy." The organization offers dual enrollment and college credit opportunities, comprehensive instructor and student resources, and high-quality content that addresses topics such as Web site design, database design, JavaScript, project management, and more. (http://www.ciwcertified.com)

Computer Professionals for Social Responsibility has a unique mission: "to promote the responsible use of computer technology."

Fast
Facts

Spanning Generations

Think the Internet is intimidating to the "older generation"? Consider the following facts, compiled by the Pew
Internet and American Life Project in 2009:

- More than half of the online population is between 18 and 44
  years old.

- Teens and users age 18 to 32 are the most likely groups to use the
  Internet for entertainment and for communicating with friends
  and family.

- People ages 33 to 44 are the most likely group to bank, shop, and
  look for health information online. These users account for 67
  percent of online banking and 80 percent of purchases made.

- People age 45 to 73 and up use the Internet less for socializing
  and entertainment and more as a tool for information searches,
  e-mailing, and buying products.

- Seventy-four percent of Internet users age 64 and older send and
  receive e-mail, making email the most popular online activity for
  this age group. Although e-mail is popular, only 73 percent of
  teens currently use it, which is down from 89 percent of teens in
  2004.

- Since 2005, the biggest increase in Internet use has been with
  people age 70 to 75. Forty-five percent of these people are currently online.

- Teen Internet users' favorite online activity is still game playing;
  78 percent of Internet users age 12 to 17 play games online, compared with 73 percent of online teens who use e-mail, the second
  most popular activity for this age group.

CPSR concerns itself with a wide range of issues, including computers and the environment, intellectual property, Internet gov-
ernance, privacy and civil liberties, technology and ethics, and
the "global information society." The group was founded in 1981,
and has helped educate policymakers and the public on a wide
range of issues. Its members have been involved in such projects

as Privaterra, the Public Sphere Project, EPIC (the Electronic Privacy Information Center), the 21st Century Project, the Civil Society Project, and the CFP (Computers, Freedom and Privacy) Conference. There is an active calendar of events, too. (http://www.cpsr.org)

Computer Security Institute is the first and leading educational membership organization for information security professionals. "At the forefront of security trends and research, CSI provides a forum for security professionals to learn, share, even debate the latest thinking on security strategies and technologies." CSI holds two conferences annually: CSI SX in spring, in conjunction with Interop, and the Annual Computer Security Conference and Exhibition in the fall. These conferences are designed for those entering the field of computers and technology, as well as experienced practitioners. (http://www.gocsi.com)

The Computing Research Association is a conglomeration of hundreds of academic departments in computer science, computer engineering, and related fields; laboratories and centers in industry, government, and academia engaging in basic computing research; and affiliated professional societies. The organization's aim is to promote education and research, as well as opportunities for women and minorities, and to provide input in policymaking. Members include universities throughout the United States, Microsoft Corporation, Palo Alto Laboratories, AT&T, Sun Microsystems, and the Society for Industrial and Applied Mathematics. (http://www.cra.org)

Graphics Special Interest Group (SIGGRAPH) might seem to have a narrow niche at first glance. The group's mission and purpose is to "promote the generation and dissemination of information on computer graphics and interactive techniques" and "foster a membership community whose core values help them to catalyze the innovation and application of computer graphics and interactive techniques." However, computer graphics play a key role in many applications, from movies to simulations and more. The site provides, among other things, important information on upcoming events and has a jobs section. (http://www.siggraph.org)

HDI Originally known as the Help Desk Institute, HDI is the "largest association for IT service and support professionals" with more than 7,500 members. As such, the organization "produces numerous publications, hosts several symposiums and two conferences each year, and certifies hundreds of help desk and service desk professionals each month." (http://www.thinkhdi.com)

IEEE Computer Society is the world's leading organization of computing professionals, with more than 85,000 members. Founded in 1946, and the largest of the 39 societies of the Institute of Electrical and Electronics Engineers (IEEE), the Computer Society is "dedicated to advancing the theory and application of computer and information-processing technology." The organization offers technical journals, magazines, conferences, books, conference publications, and online courses. Those who are switching from a different career to one in computers and programming should consider the IEEE CS Certified Software Development Professional (CSDP) program; people new to this field should consider the Certified Software Development Associate (CSDA) credential. (http://www.computer.org/portal/site/ieeecs/index.jsp)

Information Technology Association of America was created to "represent and enhance the competitive interests of the U.S. information technology and electronics industries . . . by providing leadership in business development, public policy advocacy, market forecasting and standards development to more than 350 corporate members." Members range from small start-ups to industry leaders offering services, system integration, Internet, telecommunications, software, electronics and hardware solutions to the public and commercial sector markets. (http://www.itaa.org)

Institute for Certification of Computing Professionals has dedicated itself to the "establishment of high professional standards for the computer industry." To that end, the group promotes these standards by offering certification in two major professional designations: Certified Computing Professional (CCP) and Associate Computing Professional (ACP). (http://iccp.org)

The Interactive Digital Software Association is dedicated to serving the business and public affairs needs of companies that publish video and computer games for video game consoles, personal computers, and the Internet. IDSA offers services to interactive entertainment software publishers, including a global anti-piracy program, owning the Electronic Entertainment Expo (E3) trade show, business and consumer research, government relations, and First Amendment and intellectual property protection efforts. (http://www.idsa.com)

International Webmasters Association is a nonprofit professional association with the goal of providing educational and certification standards for Web professionals. With more than 60 online, instructor-led classes and four Web certificates, IWA's accomplishments include "the industry's first guidelines for ethical and professional standards, Web certification and education programs, specialized employment resources, and technical assistance to individuals and businesses." (http://www.iwanet.org)

Internet Society is a nonprofit organization designed to "provide leadership in Internet-related standards, education, and policy." The group is dedicated to "ensuring the open development, evolution, and use of the Internet for the benefit of people throughout the world." In addition, the Internet Society is the home base for the Internet Engineering Task Force (IETF) and the Internet Architecture Board (IAB). (http://www.isoc.org/isoc)

Microsoft Certifications provides a detailed overview of the various certifications that are available, what they can do for your career, where to register, study guides, and special offers. (http://www.microsoft.com/learning/mcp/default.mspx)

National Association of the Self-Employed is a wonderful resource for those who decide to go into business for themselves (whether online or offline). The group acts as an advocate for small businesses, giving them the tools they need to succeed and thrive, and making sure that small businesses have the same benefits and opportunities as the bigger businesses out there. (http://www.nase.org)

Open Group "is a vendor-neutral and technology-neutral consortium, whose vision of 'Boundaryless Information Flow' will enable access to integrated information, within and among enterprises, based on open standards and global interoperability." (http://www.opengroup.org)

Society of Internet Professionals is a nonprofit group designed to represent the interests of Internet professionals. The group's mission is "to enhance educational and professional standards for Internet professionals." As such, SIP has created the Accredited Internet Professional (AIP) designation. (www.sipgroup.org)

Software Engineering Institute is a federally funded research and development center that has "served as a national resource in software engineering, computer security, and process improvement." The organization is part of Carnegie Mellon University and works closely with defense and government organizations, industry, and academia. (http://www.sei.cmu.edu/)

Software & Information Industry Association is the "principal trade association for the software and digital content industry. SIIA provides global services in government relations, business development, corporate education, and intellectual property protection to the leading companies that are setting the pace for the digital age." (http://www.siia.net/default.asp)

World Wide Web Consortium was created by Tim Berners-Lee to "lead the World Wide Web to its full potential by developing protocols and guidelines that ensure long-term growth for the Web." The organization pursues this mission through the creation of Web standards and guidelines. (http://www.w3.org/)

WOW Academy is committed to offering the "best Webmaster training courses, assessment exams, and certification options to meet the needs of aspiring Web professionals." (http://wowacademy .com/wowacademy/wowcertifications02.cfm)

Books and Periodicals

Whether you read bound printed books and magazines or electronically on an e-reader, the following materials will help you understand even better how the Internet came into being, where it is going, and how to maintain a career within this exciting industry.

Books

100 Top Internet Job Sites: Get Wired, Get Hired in Today's New Job Market. By Kristina M. Ackley (Impact Publications, 2000). Expands upon the material provided in Chapter 4 by explaining how to go beyond the traditional online job sites to advance your Internet career. Learn how to prepare for employment via the Internet, how to locate information about that "dream job," how to locate (and effectively use) résumé-posting Web sites, and how best to research potential employers.

The Age of Spiritual Machines: When Computers Exceed Human Intelligence. By Ray Kurzweil (Viking, 1999). A fascinating look at where computers may eventually take us. According to Kurzweil, by the year 2020, computers will have outpaced the human brain in terms of intelligence and computational power. An expert on artificial intelligence, Kurzweil postulates his "law of time and chaos" whereby technological evolution moves at an exponential pace, time speeds up as order increases, and vice versa. He believes it is possible, if not inevitable, for computer to become more conscious, and that the problems this presents need to be addressed now rather than later.

Build an eBay Business QuickSteps. By John Cronan and Carole Matthews (McGraw-Hill, 2005). Explains in concise, easy-to-follow procedures how to start and grow a successful business selling items on eBay. It is possible to make a living on eBay; this book is a great starting point for those interested in such a venture but who are perhaps new to the site and are not sure where to start.

Career Opportunities and Computers and Cyberspace. By Harry Henderson (Ferguson Books, 2004). Explains both the opportunities and challenges for those launching a career in computers and programming. This book describes careers readers can consider beyond the traditional programmer, developer, or database administrator—such as specialized librarians, manufacturing, sales, and more.

Careers in Computer Graphics and Animation. By Garth Gardner (GGC, 2001). Helps those who love art find a career on the Internet. The book provides extensive, in-depth information on specific positions, salary information, real-life stories from those professionals who have paved the way, and how to create a portfolio with pizzazz. It can be a great place to start after reading Chapter 4 in this book.

Code and Other Laws of Cyberspace .By Lawrence Lessig (Basic Books, 1999). Challenges the popularly held notion that the Internet cannot be regulated. On the contrary, Lessig argues that the Internet, the Web, cyberspace can become a more tightly controlled arena than "real life." However, we have choices in how this space is regulated, choices that this book explores.

Cyberlaw Handbook for E-commerce. By John W. Bagby (Thomson, 2003). Can help ensure that anyone starting an online business can do so legally yet successfully. It explains important legal, regulatory, and public policy issues, as well as legal and business issues relating to e-commerce. Topics include law in e-business, copyrights, trade secrets, contracts, and privacy, among others.

Database Nation: The Death of Privacy in the 21st Century. By Simson Garfinkel (O'Reilly Media, 2001). Explores in detail the predicament the world finds itself in as technology takes over more and more of people's lives—and the consequences of privacy having been largely ignored until recently. Garfinkel explores the history of identification procedures; the computerization of ID systems; how and where data is collected, tracked, and stored; and the laws that protect privacy. He also explains who owns, manipulates, ensures the safety of, and manages the vast amount of data that makes up this vast infrastructure: giant corporations that use this data to take mining to the extreme.

Electronic Brains: Stories from the Dawn of the Computer Age. By Mike Hally (Joseph Henry Press, 2005). A great book for those looking to better understand how social and historical factors shaped the history of computing. Rather than focusing on the history of the technology, however, this book concentrates more on the people. In addition, it provides information on Australian, British, American, and Soviet computer pioneers, and touches on social issues like the Cold War and IBM's business relationship with Nazi Germany.

Expert Résumés for Computer and Web Jobs. By Wendy S. Enelow and Louise M. Kursmark (JIST Works, 2005). A must-have resource for those looking to advance a career in this field, regardless of the specific area. This book is aimed directly at the Internet field, with secrets and sample résumés and cover letters for a variety of positions, from computer systems professionals to project managers to Web designers and more.

The Google Story. By David A. Vise and Mark Malseed (Delta Trade Paperbacks, 2008). Offers an in-depth look at the juggernaut that is Google, tracing the company's early days and its rise to the top of the search engine pile, to say nothing of the company's success story just from a business perspective.

How the Web Was Won: Microsoft from Windows to the Web. By Paul Andrews (Broadway Books, 1999). Explains how in 1993, when the Internet came to the forefront of popular culture, things looked bad for Windows. The Internet ran on Unix; the World Wide Web, not Microsoft Windows, was connecting the world; and a new software program called Mosaic made finding and reading Web documents easy. This book describes how Microsoft clawed its way to the lofty position it holds today—going from a relatively unknown company to a monopoly-like behemoth— and the handful of Internet devotees who led the way.

How to Be a Successful Internet Consultant. By Jessica Keyes (AMACOM, 2002). A vital book for those launching a career in

e-commerce—or for those who want to help such people be successful. Since an estimated 80 percent of small businesses do not have
Web sites, this is where the Web consultant can shine—provided
he or she has up-to-the-minute information and the most effective
tools to stay ahead of the curve. Relevant skills include both technology and business, which this book discusses in detail.

The Information Revolution. By J. R. Okin (Ironbound Press, 2005).
Provides yet another take on the history of the Internet. Some of
the information is familiar enough, but the focus of this book is
how the Web operates as a service on the Internet, enabling the
sharing of information, how organizations are using the Web,
and how the Web may evolve to meet society's changing needs.

On the Way to the Web. By Michael A. Banks (Apress, 2008). Provides a fascinating, engaging look at the "secret" history of the
Internet—so-called because these are the stories that not everyone knows about. Some of this information was provided in Chapter 1, but this book explores the Internet's history even further,
with reports on the first online privacy scandal (which actually
took place more than 30 years ago), the first instance of online
censorship in 1979, early instances of cons and identity theft, and
the wireless Internet that was built in 1978.

Smart Mobs: The Next Social Revolution. By Howard Rheingold
(Perseus Books, 2002). Takes a look at how the explosive rise
of the Internet—in particular, cell phones, PDAs, and pagers—
has allowed people from all over the world, people who may not
even know each other, to act as a cohesive group. In major cities,
Rheingold says, techno-hipsters can congregate in Wi-Fi areas
that interact with their wireless devices to let them participate in
a virtual social scene. Any parent who has watched their child
text a friend who is sitting right next to them is surely familiar
with this phenomena.

Top 100 Computer and Technical Careers. By Michael Farr (JIST
Works, 2007). Expands upon Chapters 3 and 4 of this book, including careers that might include industries readers had not previously
considered. The book also offers a job-match grid tool for those still
looking to determine a career path, advice on effective job searching, and information on trends in jobs and industries.

Tribes: We Need You to Lead Us. By Seth Godin (Penguin Group,
2008). Just may help you find and channel your inner leader.
According to Godin, tribes are groups of people aligned around

an idea, connected to a leader and to each other. They make the world work—and always have. The Web has enabled an explosion of all kinds of tribes. They are easier than ever to find, organize, and lead—and yet, not enough people are doing so. Godin believe this is the hottest growth industry today and explains why and how "tribal leaders" can emerge.

Weaving the Web: The Original Design and Ultimate Destiny of the World Wide Web. By Tim Berners-Lee (HarperCollins, 2000). A fascinating memoir, written by the man who first conceived of the World Wide Web. It details the history and philosophy behind the Internet. Berners-Lee describes how the idea for the Web came about, how it was developed, and the quantum leap in programming it launched. The release of graphical browsers such as Netscape Navigator and Internet Explorer made the Web easier for home users to navigate and led to the explosion of commercialization opportunities—the dot-com era. Berners-Lee also explains why he does not think using the Internet to make money is a bad thing, discusses issues surrounding privacy and pornography, and offers his prediction for the future of the Web.

Web Database Development Step by Step. By Jim Buyens (Microsoft Press, 2000). Written so developers can learn the skills they need to create Web databases with Microsoft .NET, including the .NET framework and Microsoft Visual Studio.NET. Whether readers are old hands at database development or new to the field, this book ensures that they are on top of new Web database development techniques.

Web of Deception: Misinformation on the Internet. Edited by Anne P. Mintz (Information Today, 2002). Provides essays from top information gurus that provide the information Internet users need to successfully navigate the Web. Topics include Web hoaxes and counterfeit sites, medical misinformation, threats to people's identity and privacy, charity scams, and more. By the end of this book, readers will know how to properly evaluate a site, how to search effectively, how to protect themselves and their families, and more.

Where Wizards Stay Up Late: The Origins of the Internet.By Katie Hafner (Simon and Schuster, 1998). Provides an in-depth look at the revolutionary science behind the creation of the Internet and the brilliant (albeit at times eccentric) scientists and engineers at universities and agencies worldwide that made it possible, with a focus on how the Cold War era led to its conception.

Periodicals

BtoB Magazine is focused entirely on marketing strategies and provides information on a wide range of topics, with tools that are designed to help strategists make the most of their advertising dollars and ensure that they get the results they expect. There is also a listing of upcoming events and even a job board. (http://www.btobonline.com)

BusinessWeek may not seem particularly relevant at first glance to someone new to the field of computers. However, with articles on technology, investing, companies, innovation, and more, the astute person may, just by paying a little attention, identify upcoming trends in this industry and take advantage of them. (http://www.businessweek.com)

Dr. Dobb's provides access to dozens and dozens of periodicals, all housed under one portal. With blogs, podcasts, newsletters, and other resources, the site is practically a one-stop shop for a wide range of information, from programming languages to databases, open-source initiatives to security. (http://www.ddj.com)

Edge is an online magazine with a broad-spectrum take on the video game industry. It includes previews of upcoming games, reviews of recently released titles, opinion columns, in-depth features, and more. (http://www.edge-online.com/magazine)

Information Week reports on those areas where business and technology collide—which means practically all aspects of a business. The magazine also provides information on upcoming events, offers marketing solutions, and more. Covered business sectors include such diverse areas as healthcare, finance, and security. (http://www.informationweek.com)

InfoWorld "identifies and promotes emerging technology segments that add unique value for the organizations that implement them, as well as the vendors that provide those solutions." The site includes "hands-on analysis and evaluation, as well as expert commentary on issues surrounding emerging technologies and products." (http://www.infoworld.com)

Linux Journal considers itself the "most trusted-source of information" for the Linux community. The magazine provides tips and tricks, in-depth tutorials, product reviews, insights from leading Linux personalities, and more. (http://www.linuxjournal.com/)

PC Gamer is a magazine available in both print and online forms. It provides reviews, how-to articles on systems and hardware, gaming news, previews, and more. (http://www.pcgamer.com/)

PC Magazine is available in both print and online forms and delivers "authoritative, labs-based comparative reviews of computing and Internet products . . . placed in the unique context of today's business technology landscape." (http://www.pcmag.com/)

PC World covers practically everything computer-related, from cell phones and PDAs, to gaming and home theaters, storage, monitors, printers, and more. There is even a section on Macintosh computers. This site provides the news and reviews users need to stay on top of IT technology. The Tech Events section provides important highlights from recent conferences and other events. (http://www.pcworld.com)

Wired magazine is available in both print and online forms and reports on how technology affects culture, the economy, and politics. (http://www.wired.com)

Web Sites

The Web sites in this section are worthy of note but do not fit into any of the other categories in this chapter. Thus, they get a category all their own. Some are practical, while others are just fun. All have the potential to further enhance an Internet-related career.

AllConferences.com is a site that provides a comprehensive list of computer-related conferences. Areas of focus include artificial intelligence, databases, mobile computing, open source, security, virtual reality, and more. (http://www.allconferences.com /Computers)

AudienceScience is designed to help users and online businesses meet and achieve success by using data mining. The company operates by using a proprietary platform to collect and measure Internet users' interests and intent by examining their Web behaviors—the sites they visit, the articles they read, the searches they make, and more. This information is then parsed and stored in massive data warehouses according to audience. By taking advantage of this service, business can reach the right people with the right message at the right time. (http://www .digimine.com)

Bored.com provides a practically never-ending source of time-wasters on the Internet. There are games, quizzes, links to a wide range of entertaining Web sites, and even some money-making ideas (although these should be taken with a grain of salt and researched thoroughly first). (http://www.bored.com)

The Games List is billed as "the world's greatest social networking site for casual gaming" and offers hundreds of games and asks readers to rate the games once they have played them. As a result, when you return to the site, you will receive game recommendations based on your preferences. Members are encouraged to add games for others to play and rate. (http://www.thegameslist.com)

Information Management serves the Internet technology and business communities by providing vital information on data management. The site is extensive, with information on business intelligence, data warehousing, data modeling, enterprise information management, and more. (http://www.information-management.com)

NetLingo calls itself "The Internet Dictionary," and while there are certainly a plethora of Internet glossaries and dictionaries on the Web, this is one of the best. Its content is extensive, with information on everything from standard terms and jargon to acronyms, abbreviations, and smileys. Subscribe to the word of the day to stay on top of what words are hot and what words are not. (http://www.netlingo.com)

SkillPath provides training and conferences for a wide range of industries, including business skills, computer skills, and more. Audio conferences and Webinars are available, as are on-site training sessions. (http://www.skillpath.com/index.html/gs/gse001)

Snopes.com is perhaps the best-known site aimed at debunking or verifying various urban legends and myths. Whether you browse the site for fun, education, or both, you will know whether passing on an e-mail about an alleged virus or Internet scam will make you look well informed or like you do not know a modem from a mouse. (http://www.snopes.com)

W3 Schools offers a wide range of training and certification in areas ranging from HTML, XML, browser and server scripting, Web building, multimedia applications, and more. (http://www.w3schools.com)

Index

W

Wall, Aaron, 35
Wal-Mart, 31
Walt Disney Company, 28
WAN. *See* wide area network
Waterfall, viii
WC3. *See* World Wide Web Consortium
Web 1.0, 12–18
    2.0 v., 18–19
Web 2.0, 16, 18–20, 130
    1.0 v., 18–19
    RSS feeds in, 19–20
wireless, 20
Web 3.0, 16, 20–21
Web cams, 42
Web Explorer, 11
webmaster, 70. *See also* Web site designers
Web producer, 70–71
Web programmer/developer. *See* Web site designers
Web server. *See* host
Web site designers, 24, 71, 90, 93
    certifications for, 88–90
    outsourcing for, 25
Web site flow architect, salary of, 71
Web sites, ix, 23, 71, 114, 119, 132, 145, 148–149
    advertising trends on, 32–33, 94–101
    growth of, 13, 14, 16
Webvan.com, 14
WebYoda's Online Webmaster (WOW) Academy, 88, 89, 142
Wendleton, Kate, 102
WHO. *See* World Health Organization
wide area network (WAN), 5, 7–8, 64–65, 135
widgetization, 18, 21

Wikipedia, 19, 20, 135
Windows Server 2008-Director, 86
Wired, 10, 11, 18–19, 148
wireless technology, 20, 42, 53
Wolfe, Gary, 10
Wolfe, Shaun, 46–48
Wolfram, Stephen, 34
Wolfram Alpha, 34
WomenTrend, 25
WordPress, 23
WordTracker.com, 100
World Health Organization (WHO), 59
World Wide Web, 1, 8, 11, 13, 18, 21, 22, 38, 118, 120, 126, 130–131, 135, 146
    business-to-business sector on, 14
    changes from, 15
    Internet compared to, 9
World Wide Web Consortium (WC3), 22, 38, 89, 135, 142
WOW Academy. *See* WebYoda's Online Webmaster (WOW) Academy

X

X.25 transmission standard, 5–6
Xbox/Xbox 360, 43, 122
XHTML, 89
XML (eXtensible Markup Language), 19–20, 132, 149

Y

"Y2K Bug," 22
Yahoo!, 33, 43–44
Yang, Jerry, 43–44
YouTube, 14, 18, 19, 23, 32, 95
    advertising links on, 20

Z

Zune, 43